A SONG FOR THE HORSES

Global Change / Global Health

JANELLE BAKER, CYNTHIA T. FOWLER, AND ELIZABETH ANNE OLSON

K. G. HUTCHINS

A Song for the Horses

Musical Heritage for More-than-Human Futures in Mongolia

THE UNIVERSITY OF
ARIZONA PRESS
TUCSON

The University of Arizona Press
www.uapress.arizona.edu

We respectfully acknowledge the University of Arizona is on the land and territories of Indigenous peoples. Today, Arizona is home to twenty-two federally recognized tribes, with Tucson being home to the O'odham and the Yaqui. Committed to diversity and inclusion, the University strives to build sustainable relationships with sovereign Native Nations and Indigenous communities through education offerings, partnerships, and community service.

ISBN-13: 978-0-8165-5567-3 (hardcover)
ISBN-13: 978-0-8165-5566-6 (paperback)
ISBN-13: 978-0-8165-5568-0 (ebook)

Cover design by Leigh McDonald
Cover art from *Days* by Urjinkhand Onon
Typeset by Leigh McDonald in Calluna 10.25/14

Library of Congress Control Number: 2024060668

Printed in the United States of America
♾ This paper meets the requirements of ANSI/NISO Z39.48-1992 (Permanence of Paper).

CONTENTS

ILLUSTRATIONS

FIGURES

TABLES

ACKNOWLEDGMENTS

The animating force of this book is the idea that hope can be found even as the end of a world looms overhead. As such, I would first like to acknowledge the two teachers who first showed me that such a hope is possible, both of whom have passed away in recent years. The first is György Kara, or as his students call him, Kara *bagsh*, the eminent folklorist who spent his life delving into counter-hegemonic world-building in the Mongolic-speaking world and who personally safeguarded no small amount of traditional spiritual knowledge and minority language and culture from the lathe of autocracy throughout the twentieth century. The second is Dad'süren Garam, the herder, singer, and cowboy philosopher who spent countless hours sharing his stories of surviving not one but two world-ending transformations on the Mongolian Gobi and who likewise safeguarded wisdom from one world into the next.

I owe a debt of gratitude to my teachers and collaborators at the Music and Dance College, especially Ganbold Muukhai, who has been a longtime friend and collaborator. Likewise, much of this research would not have been possible without the help of Khorolsüren Namkhai and the Mongolian National Philharmonic. I would like to thank my hosts in Dundgovi for their hospitality and patience during my research and those herders and musicians who participated in the project for sharing their insights and expertise with me. I would also like to thank my longtime friend

Erdenebat Jamaa for his help with questions on Mongolian Buddhism and Davaadorj Legden for helping me logistically and for our long conversations over *airag*. Above all, I could have never even attempted this research without the unequaled guidance and support of my Mongolian language teacher, Tserenchunt Legden.

The research that informs this book was produced in association with the Mongolian State University of Arts and Culture. I would like to extend my sincere gratitude to my colleagues at the MSUAC, without whom I would not have been able to carry out this research, especially Dr. Gantsetseg for helping me organize my research project, Dr. Pürevkhüü for allowing me to play in his horse fiddle orchestra, and Dr. Chuluuntsetseg for allowing me to shadow her long-song classes. I would like to thank Delgeree Choi for her patience in helping me carry out the logistic end of my research. Of course, this research would not be possible without the participation of many horse fiddle instructors and students at this institution.

The American Center for Mongolian Studies has contributed more to the long-term success of my research than any other organization, having supported my research since 2010. I would like to extend my sincerest gratitude to the former director, Robin Charpentier, as well as the longtime manager of the center, Baigalmaa Begzsüren, for helping me navigate life and research in Mongolia from early on. I would also like to thank Tsermaa for her advice and Namjaa for her humor, which I greatly appreciate whenever I travel to Mongolia.

This book is based on research I began as a graduate student at the University of Wisconsin–Madison. Dr. Zhou Yongming, who acted as my primary adviser for many years, was fundamental to my intellectual development. After taking over as my adviser and chair of my dissertation committee, Dr. Jerome Camal helped me frame my project and constantly pushed my thinking, especially at the intersection of anthropology and ethnomusicology. I would like to thank my committee members for contributing their time and expertise to help me through my academic journey. Dr. Stambach's guidance on the anthropological study of education and her support in my early career has been invaluable to me. I would like to thank Dr. Enriquez for her guidance in framing my project and her suggestions for undertaking rural music studies. Dr. Peterson inspired me to think through animals as performers, which further drove me to think through animals as critical audiences of performance, which would become a major theme in this book.

As I worked to transform this project from a dissertation to a book, I relied on the support of an expanded network of mentors. Dr. Manduhai Buyandelger has been my biggest support in furthering my research and career. Dr. Barbara J. King has been inspirational for me as I work to find my place in the world of more-than-human anthropology. Dr. Peter K. Marsh and Dr. Batjargal Badamjav have given me direction for diving more deeply into the study of Mongolian folk music.

The research for this project was made possible by support from the Fulbright-Hays Doctoral Dissertation Research Abroad Fellowship and the American Center for Mongolian Studies Cultural Heritage Fellowship. The writing and publication of this book was supported in part by a Mellon Grant through the Luce Initiative on Asian Studies and the Environment at Oberlin College and further support from Oberlin's Grant-in-Aid Fellowship. I would like my supervisors in Oberlin's LIASE program, Dr. Ann Sherif and Dr. Steve Wojtal, for their guidance and support, especially during the height of the pandemic. During this time, my friends at Oberlin Shansi, Executive Director Gavin Tritt and Senior Director Dr. Ted Samuel, offered operational support for outreach related to this project and moral support for the writing of this book. The executive director of Oberlin's grants office, Pam Snyder, and the grants coordinator, Elizabeth Edgar, both graciously and patiently helped me find and acquire grants to finish this project.

I have many people to whom I owe gratitude from my time at Oberlin College as a postdoctoral fellow and visiting assistant professor. Professors Erika Hoffman-Dilloway, Baron Pineda, Amy Margaris, and Jason Haugen from the Department of Anthropology have been incredibly generous and supportive. Conversations with Damien Droney were invaluable in helping me finish the book and get it to publication.

Some portions of this book have been previously published: parts of chapter 2 were published in *Inner Asia Journal* as "The Melodious Hoofbeat: Ungulate Rhythms in the Post-Socialist Conservatory"; an early version of chapter 3 was published in the *Journal of Ethnobiology* as "Like a Lullaby: Song as Herding Tool in Rural Mongolia"; and parts of chapter 5 were published in *Études Mongoles et Sibériennes, Centrasiatiques et*

Tibétaines under the title "With Each Pass, Another Stone: Ovoo at the Heart of Heritage, Environment, and Conflict."

I would like to thank my editor at the University of Arizona Press, Allyson Carter, and editorial assistant Alana Enriquez for their support of this project. I would also like to thank the editors of the press's Global Health / Global Change series, Dr. Janelle Baker, Dr. Cynthia Fowler, and Dr. Elizbeth Anne Olson, for their support and confidence in the project.

I have been lucky to have peers who inspire me. I would like to thank Dr. Alex MacAlvay, Dr. Bo Wang, Jeffrey Godsey, and Kendra Thomson for their friendship and support throughout graduate school at the University of Wisconsin. I would also like to thank the cohort of colleagues that I have met and worked with throughout my fieldwork, including Dr. Charlotte D'Evelyn, Dr. Marissa Smith, Sainbayar Gundsambuu, Dr. Kenny Linden, Bolor Lkhaajav, Zaya Bulag, Bazo, Javkhaa, and Dulguun Bayasgalan.

My family has been incredibly patient and supportive as I traveled to remote parts of far-off Mongolia many times over the course of the past ten years. Without the insistence of my mother, Sarah, I would never have taken up the horse fiddle in the first place. Without the intellectual support of my father, William, I would not have been inspired to pursue anthropological study. My sister Franya and nibling Lily have been supporters of me from all the way back when this project was nothing more than an empty binder labeled "BOOK." I would like to thank Sasha Madison and Babí for offering support and Vitamin C throughout my writing. None of my intellectual or creative work would be possible without the constant help, support, and inspiration from my *amin khairtai* Jessica Madison Pískatá. Jessica has been my best friend and partner throughout fieldwork and writing, and she never ceases to amaze me with her insight and intellect. I look forward to our future together and the many intellectual, poetic, and personal projects that we have yet to carry out. I would be remiss if I did not acknowledge my multispecies social relationships; as such, I would like to thank my cats, Mishka and Igor, who have contributed nothing to the writing of this book but whom I love dearly nonetheless. Finally, I would like to thank my daughter for being both a source of hope and a reason to seek hope out.

A SONG FOR THE HORSES

INTRODUCTION

In the high summer, as the cranes coasted gently back from far-off oceans, the people of Gombo's encampment planned a party. It was a *nair*—a seasonal fete that in the Mongolian Gobi consists primarily of group singing and downing silver bowls of a lightly alcoholic and effervescent drink made from mare's milk called *airag*. Traditionally, here in Dundgovi province, a *nair* begins and ends with a community elder singing a special kind of local folk song called a long-song.

For this party, three men from the county, each of them shepherds and highly regarded singers, took on the role of singing the opening song together. Dad'süren, usually referred to as "Dad' guai,"* was not the eldest, but he was the most venerated singer. He was a well-known and knowledgeable local figure, who would stroke the long mustaches that descended past his soul patch and right off his chin to the side whenever he told a story. Sitting next to Dad' guai was Buyaa akh,** wearing his signature fedora and a silver-colored *deel*. Buyaa was garrulous, but humble, always ready to jump in to extol another's virtues. His singing was colored

---

* "Sir Dad'."
** "Big Brother Buyaa."

by his ever-present smile. The eldest and most reserved of this trio was
Myagmar akh,* known for his thoughtful, craggy expression.

The three elders sang "Uyakhan Zambuu Tiviin Naran," a traditional
Gobi long-song that has come to be one of the most widely beloved songs
in the country. The term *long-song* refers not to the length of the overall
songs themselves, but from the extended ornamental phrases that singers
improvise within the melodies. The men's voices moved through the melody from long, low, sustained notes ornamented with a kind of slow vibrato unique to the genre to rapid rises that pushed higher and higher until plateauing at a haunting falsetto. They carried the weight of experience
in their voices, each in their own distinct and undeniable way. The three
men braided their performances together, their overlapping improvisa-
tions moving in and out of sync to create a polyphonic effect. Dad'süren
would later explain that the reason they sang the song differently was that
they were each picturing a different part of the Gobi landscape and tracing
their horizons with the improvisational moments in their performances.

Earlier that summer, the general mood had been grim. No one remembered it being this hot, this early before. Myagmar had taken me to
a hollow depression in the ground not far from the encampment. Flock
of sheep in tow, he told me that year after year, this patch of bare earth
had always been a seasonal lake. He said that the lake had a cycle, swelling
in the spring and serving as a water source for herds and wild animals
throughout the summer. Over the course of my prior trips to central
Mongolia from 2010 to 2017, I, too, had seen this lake dry out, bit by bit.
On that day, it was a bare patch of dusty earth, host only to a bleaching
cow skull and several vertebrae.

By the end of the summer, the feeling of doom seemed to have dissi-
pated. At the party, Dad'süren pulled out a kind of fiddle and was preparing
to play. It was a local traditional instrument with a trapezoidal body and
a slender neck leading up to a peg box carved into the shape of a horse's
head. He gently lifted the fiddle up by the neck and pulled a high-arched,
horsehair bow from where it had been hung on one of the instrument's
two large tuning pegs. Holding the body of the instrument between his
knees, he drew a bow against the fiddle's two thick, horsehair strings.

---

* "Big Brother Myagmar."

This instrument was a *morin khuur*, sometimes referred to in English as a "horse-head fiddle" for the iconic horse's head carved into its scroll. In this book, I will refer to the instrument with a translation more faithful to the original Mongolian name: the horse fiddle.

After quickly tuning the instrument, Dad'süren set off on a song that mimics the many gaits of a particular horse by pulling the bow across both strings in hoofbeat rhythms interspersed with rapid slides down the neck that produced a whinnying sound. The song was a kind of fiddle tune known as *tatlagan-ayaz* called "Jonon Khar" ("Black Horse Jonon"). His fingers danced on the side of the instrument's neck, index and thumb of his left hand pinching in on the black horsehair strings from both sides as his right hand guided the bow in a series of quick pulls and pushes. Dad'süren played a melody that traced the different moods of the Jonon Khar horse, starting forward with a short burst of syncopated hoofbeats before settling on a side-to-side trot of alternating short glissandos on the left and right string.

Having spent a few years studying the horse fiddle myself, I was familiar with the sounds of *tatlagan-ayaz*. At least, I was used to the versions taught at urban classical music institutions such as the National Conservatory. Still, I had a hard time following Dad'süren's song at points. The other guests at this nair, a group of Dad'süren's relatives and neighbors from around the county aged eight to eighty-five, seemed to follow the song easily. However, I was struggling to keep up. Some sections repeated too many times from a classical perspective. Others only partially repeated, leaving musical phrases unresolved. For most of the song, he stuck to what, to me, sounded like a relatively straightforward 6/8 rhythm. However, there were moments when the horse playing out through the song slipped away, cantering off into the steppe, represented acoustically by a quick drop in volume and a slip from a consistent time signature.

After this performance, Dad'süren told me that outside, the horses were listening to our music. Handing the fiddle to me, he warned that I should play in a way that will please the horses to hear. Before I had a chance to ask for more information, Buyaa offered to demonstrate one of his famous horse-title praise songs. Buyaa was one of the few people left in the province who remembered how to perform these songs, which celebrate the particular qualities of a winning racehorse (Luvsannorov 2015). To see him perform one out of season was a rare opportunity.

Buyaa pulled me from the felt round-tent and called out, "Someone bring me a horse! You have to be on horseback to sing this kind of song!" As Buyaa mounted one of the steeds hitched near the encampment to sing, Dad'süren added, "A herder learns life from horseback." Reins in one hand, silver bowl of mare's milk in the other, Buyaa began to sing the many praises of the horse he was riding.

Heritage and More-than-Human Futures

Those two moments of human-animal companionship from that summer stood out to me in stark contrast. The first, Myagmar and his sheep, standing in front of a dry lakebed. The loss of this water source was manageable but represented a state of ecological devastation that threatens nomadic life in the Gobi through a series of droughts, dust storms, and winter storms that get worse every year. Paired against this image was the joyful singing of Buyaa on horseback, highlighting the potential for multispecies conviviality and survival by shared appreciation of the music of the *nair*.

Returning to Ulaanbaatar that fall, I found that many of the music scholars, composers, and horse fiddle teachers I interviewed in the city supported the idea that animals were integral to the performance and transmission of traditional music. Many argued that deeply understanding livestock was vital for a good performance of the horse fiddle. Furthermore, they were anxious about what they perceived as an increasing social distance between young fiddlers and pastoral animals. The conservatories and orchestras that train and employ horse fiddlers were all urban-based institutions, designed around a Western model based on the separation of nature from culture. Concerns about this institutional distance from herds were exacerbated by the threat of ecological and economic disasters that make mobile pastoralism increasingly untenable for less well-off families, pushing people to urbanize.

The horse fiddle and long-song were the first elements to be included on the United Nations Educational, Scientific, and Cultural Organization's (UNESCO) list of Intangible Cultural Heritage for Mongolia. I will go into the politics of heritage in more detail in chapter 5. For now, what is important to know is that cultural heritage is an internationally recognized political designation that transforms traditional practices and artifacts into political capital for the state. Designation as "heritage" adds the economic value of uniqueness and a sense of national atavism to practices rendered unviable by the neoliberalization and globalization of markets, such as those associated with subsistence agriculture or pastoralism (Kirshenblatt-Gimblett 1995, 370). In this way, officially recognizing a practice as "cultural heritage" is a way to induct that practice into neoliberal modernity. This leads to the hazard that UNESCO's classification of cultural practices as Intangible Cultural Heritage transforms culture into a naturalized resource, which can then itself be extracted and exploited (Titon 2009; 9–10).

However, throughout my research I also witnessed many cases of people using cultural heritage to many different ends. Because heritage draws practices into neoliberal modernity from outside ontologies, horse fiddlers can use it to destabilize the colonial logics of postsocialist institutions that hold nature and culture as separate realms. I argue that people can and do use musical heritage to imagine more-than-human futures beyond environmental destruction and neoliberalism.

In *Decolonizing Extinction*, Juno Parreñas (2018) asks what futures might emerge if we embraced relationships with nonhuman animals based not on violent domination and colonial cruelty but on mutual vulnerability. She gestures toward the possibility of what could be called a multispecies future, a future in which the predominant relationship between humans and nonhuman animals is defined by interdependence rather than dominion. The ecologically destructive conditions of global neoliberalism push people in Mongolia to imagine these kinds of multispecies futures, in which humans have the possibility of nonextractive relations with the environment and nonhuman animals. Furthermore, the people I worked with used music to envision a future that was more than multispecies, based on interdependent and empathetic relationships between humans, nonhuman animals, plants, and other entities ranging from the land itself to the spirits of ancestors and potential beings from off-planet. To even imagine surviving the current era of climate change and neocolonialism requires a future that is more-than-human.

The performance of musical heritage has the potential for creating alternative futures to that of capitalist modernity. Between imagining alternative futures and creating them is the material reality of nonhumans such as livestock and sacred mountains themselves. I focus on more-than-human, environmental futures specifically because the people I worked with described concerns about increasing breakdowns of human relations with a whole host of nonhumans. Some, as we will see in chapter 6, went so far as to frame the future for rural Mongolians in terms of an ecological apocalypse.

To make this argument, I will examine how people imagine and build toward more-than-human futures by using musical heritage to foster and intensify relationships between humans and nonhuman animals. Human lives are interdependent with a whole host of nonhumans, like animals, plants, fungi, and so on (Tsing 2012). Myagmar, his sheep, and the desiccating landscape which hosts the dried water source form an assemblage, each of whose survival is dependent to some degree on active engagement with one another (Tsing 2013). Likewise, when Dad'süren sings or plays his fiddle, he does so as part of a more-than-human network that brings him together with the landscapes he draws on for inspiration, the people who sing along or quietly listen, and the horses on the hitching line, which he considers to be part of his audience. Understanding these more-than-human interdependent networks is vital for understanding moments of ecological crisis, as the relationships they build offer future possibilities for life in the face of the environmental breakdowns of neoliberal modernity (Tsing 2015).

Horses are the primary nonhuman animal whose perspectives will emerge throughout this book. Domestic horses appear in chapter 2, wild horses in chapter 4, and even spiritual horses make their presences known in chapter 1. However, horses, like humans, are entangled in relationships with a variety of other animals. As such, I will also be paying attention to camels and cattle in chapter 2 and sheep and goats in chapter 3. These five species of ungulates are referred to in Mongolian as the "five snouts" (*tavan khoshuu mal*) and have a special position among livestock as the key Mongolian traditional herds.

These livestock animals are what Haraway (2003) terms "companion species," whose bodies and histories are so deeply intertwined with those of their human herders that they socially coproduce one another. Horses on the Central Asian steppe, for example, only exist in their contemporary form as the result of millennia of domestication and selective breeding by humans. By the same token, the lives and histories of those people are deeply entwined with their horses. In a pastoral encampment, the sheep and the shepherd depend on one another to subsist in the harsh and changing environment of the grasslands and semi-deserts.

Following Haraway, there has been a wave of literature on domesticated species which considers the social potentials for examining relationships with domestic animals as kin-like in nature (Fijn 2011; Govindrajan 2018; Swanson, Lien, and Ween 2018). As Govindrajan (2018) points out, these kin relationships, built through individual acts of interspecies care, both affect and are affected by broader colonial politics. In this book there are moments where humans treat livestock in a kin-like manner, caring for distressed camels with familial affection (see chapter 2) and singing lullabies to baby sheep (see chapter 3). These kin-like interactions set up the foundation for the multispecies relationships that I discuss throughout the book.

However, there are also cases in this book where people use music to build relationships with animals that exceed or evade kinship. For example, in chapter 4 a group of long-song singers uses their performance to try to remind a recently reintroduced community of once-extinct wild horses how to be wild, creating a relationship based not on entanglement, but on the disentanglement of rewilding. In addition to their deeply interconnected history with humans, horses also have their own forms of sociality that exist and continue apart from human intervention (Hartigan 2020). By focusing on music, a different kind of relationship between humans and nonhuman animals emerges, as bearers of a shared heritage.

Though my focus is on interactions between humans and nonhuman animals, other nonhumans are invariably involved in these relationships as well. The landscape is not a passive backdrop to the relations that play out between humans and animals, but a network of nonliving actors in and of itself. Mountains and stones engage in human and animal lives as enigmatic, but powerful, actors similar to Marisol de la Cadena's (2015) "earth beings," entities in and of the land itself that have agency but are otherwise inscrutable. While de la Cadena's Andean earth beings are presented as inaccessible due their ontological alterity, horse fiddlers in the Mongolian context present music as a useful tool for accessing these geological entities.

As an example, in chapter 5, fiddlers and singers use long-song to entreat a holy mountain on the southern rim of Ulaanbaatar, their hometown, to intercede on their behalf against the urban ecological health crisis of air pollution. The meandering, highly melismatic melodies of long-song re-create the topography of the Inner Asian steppe (Pegg 2001, 106). Because of the deep aesthetic and moral relationship between long-song and local landscapes, herders in Mongolia perform these songs to connect with the land on an embodied, spiritual level (Yoon 2019). Taking music as a practice of translation between the wills of human beings and the wills of these more-than-natural earth beings allows us to understand how people navigate more-than-human networks that span across radical alterity.

Mongolia and the More-than-Human

Mongolia is a country in northeastern Asia, cradled between the Siberian taiga to the north and the Gobi semi-desert to the south. Its western border is marked by the Altai Mountains, while the eastern part of the country is characterized by vast grassland steppe. It was, of course, the heart of the Mongol Empire in the thirteenth and fourteenth centuries. After a couple of centuries of power struggles following the waning of the empire, it subsequently became a fringe of the Qing Empire during the seventeenth through nineteenth centuries. As the Qing Empire dissolved, the territory then became a Soviet satellite state for most of the twentieth century. Now Mongolia is sandwiched between Russia and China and experiences incredible economic and political pressure from both sides.

Mobile, nomadic pastoralism has been a significant part of regional economies on the territory now known as Mongolia since at least the third century BCE (Atwood 2004, 16). As of 2019 the National Statistics Office of Mongolia reports that the total national population of the "five snouts" of traditionally tended nomadic livestock has reached over 70 million, compared to the human population of only 3.2 million (National Statistics Office of Mongolia, n.d.). Nomadic pastoralism is a mode of economy that involves deep interdependence of human and animal, as well as active management of the health of the landscape (Humphrey and Sneath 1999).

Nonhuman animals have a social role within Mongolian pastoralist encampments that goes beyond their role as economic capital for herders. Fijn (2011) writes that livestock actively coproduce place alongside their human herders, forming what she terms the "co-domestic sphere" of the nomadic encampment. In addition to producing place, herders describe nonhuman animals as demonstrating a capacity for human-like nostalgia for their birthplace (*nutag*), contributing meaningfully to herders' social valuation of rural landscapes (Marchina 2019, 78).

The social power of livestock in Mongolian society extends to the spiritual as well. Through a Tibetan Buddhist ceremony locally called *seterlekh*, an individual livestock animal can be designated the *seter*, and dedicated to a deity (Fijn 2011, 231; Humphrey and Ujeed 2013, 237). Once consecrated, it is forbidden to ride or slaughter the animal, and it is given relative freedom of movement across the pasture. In return, the animal acts as a living connection between the family who "sacrificed" it and the deity to which it was dedicated. The *seter* animal is expected to use this connection to protect the rest of its herd (Fijn 2011, 231), as well as to bring the family prosperity and fertility (Humphrey and Ujeed 2013, 237).

Because of the long tradition of mobile pastoralism, livestock animals, especially the five snouts, have become symbols of Mongolian culture both locally and globally. In both socialist and postsocialist Mongolia the state used the figure of horses and horsemen to represent the nation (Bulag 1998). Myadar (2011) argues that the image of the man on horseback tending to flocks of livestock, the "imaginary nomad," has become a symbol of Mongolian rural life both for nationalists within the country and for Westerners seeking an orientalized, exotic other to consume through tourism.

The use of the horse as a symbol for a new, modern, masculine Mongolian nation is emblematized on the horse's head carving on the fiddle itself. Two to four stringed fiddles were common in premodern Mongolia with a wide variation of head carvings including not only a whole host of animals, but also demons, Buddhist symbols, and mythical astrological creatures like the *matar* ("leviathan") and *matar-zögii* ("bee-leviathan") (Pegg 2001; Danzan 2007). The contemporary horse fiddle was standardized and mobilized by the Mongolian People's Party in the twentieth century through newly established musical institutions as the symbol of a socialist, cosmopolitan nation (Marsh 2009).

Landscapes and their physical features have their own special roles in Mongolian society. As both Sneath (2014) and Madison Pískatá (2021b) show in their examinations of national sacrifices to sacred mountains, landscape features participate in the local social lives of their surrounding areas as well as the political functioning of the Mongolian state at large. Far from disenchanting the land, breakages from traditional relations with mountains, like the widespread introduction of industrial mining, have intensified encounters between humans and earthbound spirits (High 2017). Active management of relations with spirits is vital to survival in Mongolia, as the country recovers from successive eras of political upheaval (Buyandelger 2013).

What happens when the ecosystem you depend on changes radically—or worse, disappears? For the musicians and herders I worked with, this is a very real and immediate concern. While they have a large body of communal knowledge on steppe stewardship to draw on, the neoliberal world is not well suited to nomadic ways of living. I argue that heritage provides a way for people to reimagine relationships with nonhumans in the face of ecological breakdown.

There is a danger inherent to ecological anthropology of reducing native people to "ecologically noble savages," who are dehumanized by the rhetorical assertion that they are more in tune with nature by virtue of being non-Western (Redford 1991). This potential is especially worthy of scrutiny in Mongolia where orientalism and European fears of the "nomadic war machine" intermingle with Western desires for an idealized, imaginary nomadic society which is perfectly harmonized with the land (Myadar 2011). Furthermore, taking relationships between humans and nonhuman animals as culturally determined has the potential to overwrite the fact that the lives and histories of nonhuman animals are also entangled with the political legacies of colonialism (Govindrajan 2018; Parreñas 2018) and industrialization (Blanchette 2020).

If I take Dad' guai and Buyaa as experts in the arts of survivance, it is not because I consider them to have been born "closer to nature." Mongolian people, like all people, have ambivalent and contextual relationships with nonhuman animals affected by political and historical conditions (Terbish 2023). People in Mongolia have the capacity to engage in ecologically violent behavior like anyone else (Linden 2021). Throughout this book, I present cases where Mongolian approaches to ecosystem management are nascent, experimental, and subject to in-community disagreement and negotiation.

The reality is that people in northern Asia, herders and nonherders alike, have been charged with living in a landscape that is susceptible to some of the earliest dangers of climate change and ecosystem breakdown. Despite millennia of productive land stewardship by local nomads, global warming is causing rapidly increasing desertification in the Gobi (Rosen et al. 2019). Rising temperatures and widespread wildfires destroy permafrost ecosystems throughout Siberia, including Mongolia's northern mountains (Munkhjargal et al. 2020). Increasing cycles of drought and snowfall lead to winter disasters called *zud*, which kill off massive amounts of livestock and are increasingly difficult for herders to recover from because of the vulnerability that the neoliberal withdrawal of a state security net has caused (Janes and Chuluundorj 2016). This state of affairs is further exacerbated by exploitative, neocolonial relationships between Mongolia and both Russia and China, the modern incarnations of the country's two most recent colonizers. In the face of all of this, the Mongolian people I talked to over the course of this research used cultural heritage to envision more-than-human futures and work toward resilience.

Animals, Music, Modernity

Throughout this book, nonhuman animals participate in the performance and transmission of musical heritage. The materiality of musical instruments depends on resources from nonhumans, bringing the human performer into contact with elements drawn from horses and trees, which I will discuss further in chapter 1. Singers perform for horses in chapter 4 and fiddlers learn to improvise music according to their gaits in chapter 2. In chapter 3, herders pay attention to their sheep's responses to their singing, taking the livestock as critical audiences for their music. Beyond living entities, nonliving nonhumans, especially ghosts and sacred mountains, also participate alongside their living counterparts in chapters 5 and 6.

Nonhuman animals and other living beings actively participate in world-making (Tsing 2015, 22). They are capable of creating meaning through their interactions with other beings (Kohn 2013, 83–84). They are even capable of creating narratives through their repeated interactions with a place (Van Dooren and Bird Rose 2012). In the face of ecological and financial precarity, building and mobilizing more-than-human networks of relation is vital for humans and nonhumans alike (Tsing 2015). For the people I worked with, surviving environmental breakdown meant creating strong, interdependent relationships with livestock animals and with the land to identify and mitigate upcoming disasters.

Music has a unique ability to transcend barriers between humans and nonhumans, bringing humans and animals into each other's social worlds (Seeger 1987). Sound is an embodied, multisensory way to engage with a place and the total field of more-than-human entities that form it (Feld 1996). Music is an affective practice that is accessible to animals other than humans (Martinelli 2009). As a form of traditional ecological knowledge, music can even be a valuable resource for ecosystem management (Titon 2009).

Despite the fact that horse fiddle teachers generally consider animals to be important for their craft, horses and their ungulate cousins have been all but extricated from music education. This is an area of major concern for the horse fiddle teachers in chapter 2, who worry that their urban-based students will not be able to improvise with the sounds of horses and geological features—core aspects of the performance of *tatlagan-ayaz* and long-song, respectively. Conservatories, like all institutions in the postsocialist world, are the result of two successive colonial modernizing projects meant to reproduce Europe on a global scale.

Colonial modernity is built on two fundamental ideological separations. The first is the separation of culture, the realm of humans and human creations, from nature, the realm of nonhuman animals and other living beings (Descola and Sahlins 2014). The second is the separation of the West from Others, distinguishing the residents of colonial metropoles from vilified and romanticized aliens against whom Europeans could define themselves (Said 1979; Trouillot 2003). These two ideologies overlap in that European imperial powers use the dehumanization of their Others in Asia, Africa, and the Americas to justify colonial expansion.

The distinction between nature and culture is important to the modernist project not because it imagines the two as discrete, but because it sets up nature as something that can be controlled and exploited. Rather than multispecies relationality and interdependency, this ideology promotes dominion. This is the basis for the politics of perpetual growth that was at the heart of environmental destruction in both the Soviet and Capitalist paradigms that Mongolia has been subjected to since the beginning of the twentieth century.

The musical practices I outline are incompatible with neoliberal modernity because they acknowledge and depend on an entanglement of humans and other animals that does not fit within this model of the division of nature and culture. The musicians I profile take nonhuman animals and even some nonliving nonhumans as teachers, consumers, and bearers of shared heritage. Horses, mountains, and ghosts are taken as having similar musical capacities to humans through their roles in transmitting and consuming cultural heritage.

As citizens of a postsocialist former Soviet satellite state, Mongolian people first experienced global capitalism in its early neoliberal form in the 1990s. Under conditions of neoliberal modernity, people in power strive to homogenize and rationalize society (Harvey 1989). This totalizing homogenization is at odds with capitalist modernity's dependence on existence of what Trouillot terms its native "Others" and external "Elsewheres" (2003). As such, modernity creates what he calls "alter-natives," other modernities that exist alongside and in opposition to the global colonial hegemony of the West. Cultural heritage is a mechanism for creating alter-natives in the neoliberal era, as it transforms cultural differences into exploitable, national resources.

However, there may be an emancipatory potential for people to use heritage as a way of transforming their conditions from within modernist institutions. This potential exists in the interplay between imagining entangled more-than-human cultural practices and engaging with the material lives of nonhumans. Through the designation of cultural practices as "heritage," people operating under the conditions of neoliberalism invite the creation of neoliberal modernity's internal "Others." The incorporation of difference into postsocialist institutions that people achieve through the mobilization of heritage creates contexts in which those people can build toward more-than-human futures beyond modernity.

Place and Method

My research takes me across two sites in Mongolia: Ulaanbaatar and Dundgovi province. Both places have central, but different, roles in heritage administration in the country. In Ulaanbaatar the music schools, concert halls, and orchestras established as part of the socialist project maintain a central role in the transmission, performance, and administration of musical heritage. Ulaanbaatar operates as a central hub, drawing musicians and music students from around the country to pursue careers as professional performers of traditional music. Dundgovi, on the other hand, is the home of the most famous and widely beloved long-song singer, Namjilyn Norovbanzad. Through her and a few other famous musicians that have called the province home, the Dundgovi sound has become the standard long-song aesthetic taught at conservatories in the capital.

Ulaanbaatar sits on the Tuul river in central Mongolia, in a bowl formed by four sacred mountains. It would be hard to overstate the centrality of Ulaanbaatar to Mongolian society. Originally established as the seat of religious power in the seventeenth century, Ulaanbaatar has been the capital of independent Mongolia since 1924 (Atwood 2004). It is by far the largest city in the country. The Mongolian National Statistics Office reports that the city housed a population of over 1.4 million people as of the end of 2018, nearly half of the total population of the country (National Statistics Office of Mongolia, n.d.). Ulaanbaatar was the center of socialist Mongolia's national music project during the twentieth century, housing the Music and Dance College and the National Philharmonic. It has maintained this central role in the postsocialist era, as the main node in the newly privatized music industry.

To fly into Ulaanbaatar in the winter is to descend into a cauldron of purple smoke. Throughout that season, the city deals with some of the worst air pollution in the world due to the way it traps the smoke coming from small homesteads that have to burn coal to stave off the brutal cold (Hasenkopf 2012). The population of Ulaanbaatar is rising rapidly, with more people driven to settle in the city whenever a winter *zud* hits and kills off large portions of livestock, making pastoral life more and more untenable in rural parts of the country. As the population of Ulaanbaatar increases, the dual ecological catastrophes of *zud* and air pollution are exacerbated by the disastrous everyday functioning of the neoliberal state, which is incapable of providing services, including non-coal-based heating, to a rapidly increasing urban population.

Dundgovi is a mostly rural province in south-central Mongolia. The grassy steppe in the north transitions to the semi-arid steppe of the Gobi to the south. Though long-song is performed throughout Mongolia and Inner Mongolia (Yoon 2013), Dundgovi has a particular place as the home of Namjilyn Norovbanzad, the performer who brought long-song to the international stage in the mid-twentieth century. Her style, tied intimately with the Dundgovi landscape, has since become the standard among

Ulaanbaatar-based long-song instructors. It is also the home of Dad'süren, Buyaa, and Myagmar, and the setting for the *nair* that set this project into motion.

Desertification and drought are major sources of concern for people in Dundgovi. Though there are no active mines in the particular county where I worked most closely, there are active mines throughout the Gobi, and their ecological effects bring the true desert further and further north each year. Mines, and the unpaved roads that connect them to the metropoles where their resources are bought and sold, also produce dust that disrupts the health of people and pastures throughout the region (Jackson 2015). For Dad'süren and Buyaa, who base their performances of long-song on the ecological and aesthetic layout of their steppe homeland, this desertification has troubling indications for their musical heritage as well as their livelihoods.

This book is based on twenty months of ethnographic fieldwork. I draw on semi-structured interviews and participant-observation at conservatories, concerts, and other traditional music contexts like *nair*. In keeping with my research's focus on music, I used ethnomusicological methods as well. Drawing on literature that addresses the research potential of music apprenticeship (Hood 1960; Rice 2003; Hahn 2007; Bizas 2014), I enrolled in courses with a private horse fiddle teacher and played accompaniment with long-song vocal courses at the University of Arts and Culture. Inspired by Wong's (2008) use of group musical performance as a distinct kind of autoethnographic method, I joined the University of Arts and Culture's Horse Fiddle Ensemble, participating in rehearsals and performances. These experiences allowed me to reflect on my own role as a student and performer through my own experiences learning the instrument.

Though I interviewed many people throughout my time in Mongolia, in this book I will present quotations from a few key individuals. Each of these people have unique and complicated relationships with cultural heritage, but at the same time, their perspectives represent larger discourses that I found in my research writ broadly. In addition to Buyaa, Dad'süren, and Myagmar, I bring in Byambaa and Mandaa, cousins who tend to their family's herds of livestock, whose words stand in for the many ideas that herders in Dundgovi province expressed about the role of music in nomadic pastoralism. The voices of horse fiddlers like Muukhain Ganbold, an outgoing and garrulous instructor at a conservatory in Ulaanbaatar who grew up in a rural nomadic encampment in the Altai Mountains, and a fiddler I will call Tüvshee, a fellow conservatory professor whose eclectic and ostentatious manner of dress belies his humble and shy character, represent some of the many ways fiddlers conceptualize their relationship with their instrument. The concerns of people who are not themselves musicians but nonetheless have an interest in the transmission of cultural heritage are encapsulated by the dogged determination of retired engineer turned patron of the arts, Chuluun, and the grim, but hopeful, humor of the music theorist Tuyaa.

Despite the fact that this project took me around the country, I do not consider my research multisited. Throughout the course of my research, I stayed within a fairly tight community of musicians, heritage bearers, and pastoralists. In practice, few people in Mongolia are fully "settled" or fully "nomadic." For the most part, people spend some of the year in cities and towns, and the rest of the year in rural pastures. As such, I followed friends and hosts and they went about their normal yearly cycles. These cycles involved staying in rural Dundgovi during the spring to help with pastoral labor and in the early fall to participate in *nair* and staying in Ulaanbaatar during the winter and early summer to follow the normal operation of conservatories and the National Philharmonic.

Structure of Chapters

In this book I will describe several cases of human performers using musical heritage to connect with nonhumans as a way of imagining more-than-human futures beyond neoliberal modernity. In chapter 1, I examine how the horse fiddle brings humans, animals, and the land into relation with each other through the performance of the instrument. Chapters 2, 3, and 4 will focus on how human performers use heritage as a form of relating to nonhuman animals, creating an embodied sense of interspecies empathy through music. Chapters 5 and 6 then consider how performers use heritage to appeal to a larger network of nonhumans, including ghosts and landscape features such as holy mountains. Whether these appeals are accepted by their intended audience is uncertain, indicating that ambiguity will be a fundamental part of building more-than-human relations in the face of the current climate crisis.

Chapters 1 and 2 will focus on the horse fiddle itself. Chapter 1 follows a common thread from my interviews, that the horse fiddle is "an instrument with its own soul" (*sünstei khögjim*). Its chords and bowstring must be made with the hair of a living horse, creating a sympathetic link between fiddle, horse, and human performer. This connection is what forms the soul of the fiddle. Through this spirit, the fiddle grants humans access to the world of ungulates, as herders use the instrument to calm horses and coax mother camels to nurse their calves.

Chapter 2 focuses on how urban musical institutions, particularly the University of Arts and Culture's Music Department and the National Horse Fiddle Ensemble, have been transformed from their Soviet-style formation through interactions with pastoralism and herd animals that have aesthetic importance for the performance of traditional and classical music. Performers of the horse fiddle often claim that in order to play the instrument in an emotionally evocative way, the fiddler must have an intimate knowledge of rural landscapes and an ability to empathize with livestock animals. However, to be a professional horse fiddler in Mongolia involves considerable engagement with urban institutions, from the conservatories that give fiddlers' their accreditation to the orchestras and ensembles that employ them. This chapter explores the various methods that musicians, composers, and music teachers use to manage what they see as an increasing gap in this pastoral knowledge among urban performers, and how those strategies transform institutions through interactions between institutional heritage and pastoral, multispecies musical engagement.

Moving from the urban institution to the rural pasture, chapters 3 and 4 focus on the vocal performance of long-song. In the third chapter, I describe the application of song as a herding tool in Dundgovi province. The livestock birthing season in early spring is a crucial time for both humans and nonhuman animals. While pastoralists throughout the country have many different approaches for managing the challenges they face during this time, herders in Dundgovi have a special set of tools for adopting orphaned livestock to new mothers: species-specific, semi-improvisational songs. These songs are herders' primary method for instigating nursing and developing parental bonds between orphaned newborns and foster mothers. In this chapter, I take instances of livestock-singing in the Gobi as opportunities for the creation of mutual empathy between herder and animal. These performances implicate humans in the emotional worlds of sheep and give sheep the role of audiences of music—a position usually reserved for humans.

Chapter 4 follows a group of long-song singers as they travel to Hustai National Park, just outside of Ulaanbaatar, to sing for a population of wild horses. These diminutive equines, known as *takhi* or Przewalski's horses, were once nearly extinct in central Mongolia before being repopulated by concerted natural heritage conservation efforts throughout the 1990s and early 2000s. This chapter examines how a group of long-song singers empathized with the *takhi* as a community of fellow postsocialist subjects and used their singing in an attempt to forge cross-species bonds with them. In this chapter, the performers entangle cultural and natural heritage through their music to welcome the *takhi* back to the steppe. By positioning the *takhi* as a critical audience of long-song, the performers open up the category of "heritage bearer" to nonhuman actors.

Chapters 5 and 6 fold in other forms of cultural heritage that are interconnected with the fiddle and long-song, particularly land-based spiritual traditions. These chapters widen the scope to consider how nonliving nonhumans, from holy mountains to ghosts to extraterrestrials, participate in heritage. In chapter 5, I present three stories about humans engaging these more-than-human networks by interacting with *ovoo*, spiritually significant piles of stone that adorn natural heritage sites. In this chapter, I follow a hunting guide, a fiddler, and a singer. Each of these three is a bearer of traditional cultural heritage, and they balance their spiritual responsibilities to the sacred landscape with their need to participate in cultural and touristic industries to survive in Mongolia's new neoliberal economy.

The sixth chapter examines an assertion made by a music professor named Tuyaa that the Mongolian world had already ended and been rejuvenated once before. In this chapter, I argue that this apocalyptic thinking is a useful lens for approaching the Anthropocene in postsocialist societies. For Tuyaa, late capitalism and the global ecological disasters it promises are framed as another installment of a cycle of world-ending events tied to global, colonial modernist movements. Throughout this chapter, I explore cases in which musical entanglements with animals and extraterrestrials operate as avenues of recovery for people who face the prospect of a world on the edge of collapse, informed by personal, familial, and cultural memories of worlds that ended recently.

Conclusion

Each of the following chapters presents a case in which a more-than-human social interaction is vital to the performance of horse fiddle, long-song, or both. In these cases, the music is also vital to sustaining inter-species relations. Though my focus is on nonhuman animals, musical interactions between humans and horses depend on broader more-than-human networks that include sacred mountains, ghosts, and others. The horse fiddle itself, taken as a being with its own "flesh, blood, and soul," is part of this more-than-human community.

The designation of the horse fiddle and long-song as "cultural heritage" brings those cultural practices into modernity without rationalizing them completely. Heritage ascribes value to the aspects of these musical per-formances that do not fit well within neoliberal modernity. Horses and ghosts do not typically have a place as teachers or consumers of music in modernist institutions, built as they are on the fundamental premise of the secular separation of nature from culture. As heritage, horse fiddle music brings considerations for nonhumans that would otherwise fall under the category of "nature" into institutions, the realm of "culture."

Throughout this book, I present the perspectives of musicians, herd-ers, and heritage bearers. In each of the cases that follow, these heritage bearers work toward creating alternatives to modernity from within mod-ern institutions, using modernist bureaucracies. Heritage is the key to building these alternatives because it allows people to forge more-than-human relationships that challenge the nature/culture binary underpin-ning modernity.

To imagine a more-than-human future that persists beyond the current era of intensifying climate change requires us to ask a few what-ifs. What if animals can be critical consumers of music? What if they can even bear heritage? Taking animals and others seriously as participants in the mu-sical worlds of humans opens space for us to imagine a future where the violent, colonial ordering of the world is not taken for granted as the only possible way of engaging with the environment.

As the sun set, Dad'süren, Buyaa, and Myagmar closed out the *nair* with another long-song. The song they chose is officially called "Övgön Shuvuu Khoyor," "the Old Man and the Bird." In Dundgovi, people tend to call long-song by the first couple of words of the first verse. So, Dad'süren referred to this song as "Jargaltain Delger," "Expanding Joy," after the first line *"jargaltain delger zuunykhaa sard n'"* ("in the summer months of expanding joy"). Dad'süren would later explain that throughout the lyrics of this song, the old man is visited season after season by a migratory crane. Each time it comes to visit, the crane asks why the old man does not come with him, where life is easy and without the pains of living on a harsh landscape in an aging body. Where the crane would take him is left open to interpretation. Is it oblivion? Or greener pastures? Dad'süren changed his mind on this often, but he was certain of one thing. When the man was ready to go, the bird would be waiting for him.

CHAPTER 1

GHOSTS IN THE FIDDLE

The way to Ulaanbaatar's main philharmonic hall is tricky to find. I started at the city's central square, where the statues of Mongolia's socialist hero Sükhbaatar and imperial hero Chinggis Khaan face off. It was called Sükhbaatar Square the first time I visited in 2010, but the Democratic Party majority government changed it to Chinggis Square in 2013. In 2016, after the Mongolian People's Party retook control of the legislature, they changed the name back to Sükhbaatar, part of ongoing tension between the socialist nostalgia of the Communist party and the premodern nostalgia of the pro-capitalist party.

On the east side of Ulaanbaatar's central square there is an opera theater, neoclassical and pink, fronted with eight white pillars. It was built in 1963 and still hosts operas including *Uchirtai Gurvan Tolgoi** and *Eugene*

---

* Alternatively translated as "Three Fateful Hills" or "Three Fateful Characters," *Uchirtai Gurvan Tolgoi* was originally a stage play written by the luminary Mongolian author Dashdorjiin Natsagdorj in 1934, later adapted into an opera by the writer and scholar Tsendiin Damdinsüren with a score composed by Bilegiin Damdinsüren in 1942. Since then it has been a mainstay of Mongolian opera.

*Onegin** to this day. The next building over is the *Soyolyn Töv Örgöö*** which houses the Classical Art and Academic Theater and the Mongolian Theater Museum. Like the opera theater, it is in neoclassical style. It is a piece of socialist-era architectural heritage in the form of a long, white hall with gold trim and a row of stark, square columns.

The *Soyolyn Töv Örgöö* is also the home of the Mongolian National Philharmonic and its traditional music ensemble, the *Mongol Ulsyn Morin Khuuryn Chuulg.**** While the philharmonic performs in the concert halls reachable through the building's front doors, the institution itself can only be accessed through an unassuming side door, tucked behind an awning and past a security guard station. Here is where I met Khosbayar Zagdsüren and Khorolsüren Namkhai, or Khosoo and Khorloo, the Horse Fiddle Ensemble's power couple. Khorloo is the foreign affairs officer for the State Ensemble and Khosoo, her husband, is the artistic repertoire director for the Mongolian National Philharmonic. In addition to their organizational roles, they are both instrumentalists as well, Khorloo a flutist and Khosoo a horse fiddler. In their roles as artistic director and foreign affairs officer, they are charged with representing the meaning behind the music of the horse fiddle domestically and abroad.

Before I had a chance to ask my prepared questions, Khosbayar posed his own. He pulled out a horse fiddle from behind his desk and asked, "Do you know what UNESCO calls this?" He gently cradled the body in his right hand and turned the instrument back and forth by rolling the neck between his left index finger and thumb. Khorolsüren gave me the answer, "*Biyet büs soyol*, culture without a body." This is the Mongolian translation for UNESCO's category of Intangible Cultural Heritage.

---

* *Eugene Onegin*, an adaptation of the novel by Alexander Pushkin of the same name, was composed by Pyotr Tchaikovsky in the mid-nineteenth century and first performed on stage in Moscow in 1879. Throughout the twentieth century, the music of Tchaikovsky represented Russian culture and, by extention, Soviet modernity for Mongolian performers. These ideas have held over until today, as Tchaikovsky is a common presence both on the stage at Ulaanbaatar's main opera theater and in the curriculum at the city's most prominent conservatories.

** "Central Cultural Palace."

*** "Mongolian State Horse Fiddle Ensemble."

Alongside the lists of "tangible" cultural heritage and natural heritage, UNESCO keeps lists of intangible cultural heritage in need of safeguarding. While tangible heritage includes mostly architectural and archaeological sites, intangible cultural heritage is a catchall for cultural practices, especially the arts. Despite the "intangible" tag, this category also often includes the implements people use to create these arts, including musical instruments.

Khosbayar continued, holding the fiddle aloft:

> It has a body! If I break this one today, I will need a new one tomorrow. There is no music without it. The body is an important aspect of the instrument. Though, if someone plays it and does not feel it in the heart, does not play with the spirit of the fiddle, then it is just a body with no soul.

Here Khosbayar used the word *süns*, which I have translated as the "spirit" of the instrument. This term came up in many of my interviews with horse fiddle players. Fiddlers mentioned this term multiple times as a key feature of the fiddle's ability to connect humans with nonhumans. A common explanation goes as follows: The fiddle's chords and bow strings can only be made from the hair of a living horse, never from a deceased one. The body is made with wood, and rosin with sap from a tree, taken from the land. When a person plays it, they animate the instrument with their emotional force. Together these elements give a kind of living energy to the object. The cooperation of living elements involved in the construction and performance of the fiddle gives the instrument a "*süns*."

Süns can be a slippery term to translate into English. It can mean soul or spirit. *Süns* can also mean "ghost" when referring to haunted buildings. However, each of these terms has a different meaning in practice. When I asked musicians what the *süns* of the fiddle was, I received a variety of different answers. Generally, the replies fell into three categories, understanding the *süns* either as a shamanic soul, a Buddhist nature spirit, or as a New Age vibration. Regardless of how the term is understood, the *süns* of a fiddle is consistently described as an encapsulation of the material bodies involved in the performance of the music. As the fiddler Baatar put it, "the fiddle has its own body, its own blood, hair, and soul."

Throughout this book, I will present cases in which people use cultural heritage to imagine other ways of being that mobilize more-than-human networks of relation. However, these imaginaries can only be made real when the body and soul are reintegrated into the process. The body of the fiddle is a more-than-object body, its hairs connecting it to the body of a living horse and its acoustic self only possible through the movements of a human performer. This is where the *süns* is formed—at the intersection of humans, horses, and spirits.

As I have gestured to above, the designation of a cultural practice as "heritage" adds capitalistic value to lifeways that are otherwise incompatible with neoliberalism (Kirshenblatt-Gimblett 1995). The politics of heritage subsumes aspects of Mongolian political, economic, and social life that otherwise do not have a place in neoliberal capitalism, such as nomadic pastoralism or praise songs for local mountains, within the logic of capital. Capitalism is alienating, so the process of defining horse fiddle music as heritage involves disentangling the practice from the multispecies, nonsecular network of relations that gives the fiddle its particular power and thereby denying the music its body and spirit.

There is the potential for state actors to use heritage as a way of establishing and maintaining state hegemony. Governments often use the politics of heritage to transform outmoded lifeways into national power (Lowenthal 1996). The nationalization of culture through heritage is reflected in competition between states to claim certain elements on their own lists.

Nonetheless, for the musicians that I worked with the rhetorical embrace of heritage gave them an opportunity celebrate, interrogate, and analyze the entanglement of human and nonhuman lives in countermodern ways. Through this examination, they were able to imagine and build toward more-than-human futures beyond modernity. For horse fiddlers like Khosbayar, the future-making potential of the instrument can only be realized if the *soyol*, the culture, is reentangled with its *biye* and *süns*, its body and soul. For the cultural heritage to have power, it must be reintegrated with its full, animal body. The horse must be brought into the conservatory, because postsocialism's modernities rely on the separation of human from animal and of social from spiritual.

The Soul of the Fiddle

In this chapter, I focus primarily on perspectives from three horse fiddle experts based out of music institutions in Ulaanbaatar: Ganbold, Tüvshee, and Tuyaa. Ganbold is a horse fiddle performer and teacher in his late forties. He was born and raised in rural pastures in the Altai Mountains of western Mongolia before coming to Ulaanbaatar as a young man to pursue a career in music. By the time he arrived for training at what was then called the Music and Dance College (now the National Conservatory), he was already a skilled horse fiddle player, having learned several horse-gait mimicry songs and dance tunes from his mother.

Tüvshee is a little bit older than Ganbold, in his mid-fifties. He teaches the horse fiddle at the Arts and Culture University, specializing in classical music and long-song. When I first interviewed him, he was sporting a pompadour hairdo and a leopard-print silk shirt. He was one of the first musicians to try blending the horse fiddle with electronic music, performing synth-heavy remixes of mid-twentieth-century neo-traditional compositions by composers like B. Sharav and N. Jantsannorov. Now he uses his expertise to supplement the income he makes as a music teacher with a small, family-run electronics business.

Tuyaa is a musicologist and music theory teacher. In our first interview, she referred to herself as, above all else, a *khödöö össön khün* ("person raised in the countryside") and a *geodeterminist* ("geo-determinist"). She was raised in the steppes of rural far eastern Mongolia. When she originally came to Ulaanbaatar to follow her dream of becoming a professional horse fiddler, she was turned away. The primary horse fiddle teacher at the Music and Dance College at the time refused to accept female students, based on a now widely rejected idea that performing certain genres of traditional music, like horse fiddle and polyphonic throat singing, was dangerous to women's reproductive health. So instead, she traveled to the Soviet Union to continue her education in music studies before returning to teach at the institution that had once rejected her.

All three of these people live and work in Ulaanbaatar, the capital and largest city in Mongolia. They all work at national musical education institutions. As such, their perspectives on aggregate represent a distinctly urban, higher education, institutional field of view. Working through conservatories, their primary access to the horse fiddle (and all the more-than-human potential it brings with it) is through its institutionalized form as a heritage object. There are, of course, qualitative distinctions within this social class as gender, ethnolinguistic background, and rural or urban background are distinctions that make differences in these three people's lives.

Throughout the course of my research, I have interviewed dozens of fiddlers from around Mongolia. While each performer has a unique and idiosyncratic relationship with the instrument, a few broader patterns emerged in my interviews, especially regarding the horse fiddle's *süns*. I present Ganbold, Tüvshee, and Tuyaa's perspectives in this chapter not only because these three individuals speak eloquently on the topic of the horse fiddle's *süns*, but furthermore because their explanations each encapsulate one of the primary schools of thought that came through in my interviews with other performers. These different, though sometimes overlapping, epistemological orientations toward the fiddle's soul reflect broader discourses in the spiritual awakening of postsocialist Mongolia.

In each of the three explanations below, the *süns* is a by-product of the horse fiddle's mediation between human and nonhuman actors within the network of musical heritage performance. However, each of these three individuals identifies a different network. In Ganbold's version, the fiddle mediates the horse and human, creating a hybrid spirit for both in the process. In Tüvshee's explanation, the horse fiddle mediates for a much larger network that includes all the actors who contributed materially in some way to the fiddle's construction and performance, including the human musician, the horse who provides the hair, and the trees who provide the wood and rosin. Tuyaa, however, describes the fiddle's body as mediating between the musician and the fiddle itself, as the fiddle's body is what produces the *sünsleg avia* ("spiritual sound") and generates positive energy for the fiddler.

Many of the musicians I worked with, mostly cosmopolitan urbanites by nature of how the music industry operates, were uncomfortable with expressing overtly spiritual opinions directly. Ganbold elaborated in depth on his personal cosmological beliefs, which had clear throughlines with both Tengriism and Tibetan Buddhism, but he would not name his beliefs as belonging to a spiritual tradition. Tüvshee was happy to describe his practice of Buddhism, but he practices alone, in private, away from monasteries. Tuyaa directly challenged the nonsecular framing of the fiddle as *sünstei* ("with a spirit"), offering instead *sünsleg aviatai* ("with a spiritual sound").

Operating out of a conservatory in the capital city, where both socialist and neoliberal modernist thought are foundational to the institution, many musicians and music teachers are interested in the ways nature and culture are entangled but are nervous about the risk of coming off as uneducated. This sentiment came through particularly in interviews with people who had left rural pastoral communities to pursue their music career in Ulaanbaatar. As Indigenous performers of a musical tradition tied closely to nomadism, Mongolian fiddlers are exposed to multiple overlapping dehumanizing discourses. Like other Indigenous people around the world, they risk being caricatured as "ecologically noble savages," who are seen as having been born closer to nature and by extension are treated as less human (Redford 1991). They also risk being cast by sedentary people as time-lost barbarians of diminished personhood through the figure of the "imaginary nomad" (Myadar 2011). Because many Mongolian musicians have to find work outside of the country, moving to international cosmopolitan nodes, especially Beijing and Berlin, many performers feel extra pressure to combat negative stereotypes that paint Mongolians as parochial or "backward."

Because of the pressures to appeal to the post-Enlightenment rationalist division of nature and culture to avoid derision, Mongolian musicians take care in how they frame their descriptions of their interactions with nonhumans. Designation as cultural heritage allows for these musicians to use the language of folklore, of transmission via tradition and communal ownership, to speculate on spiritual topics without risking being seen as anti-modern. For example, I interviewed a horse fiddle player and luthier with the National Philharmonic of Mongolia who told me, "This is not ratified research, but people say that in order to be a good horse fiddle player you must be honest. If you are dishonest, the fiddle will not sound." In this quote, he provided a moral explanation for a physical attribute of the instrument that provides the fiddle with agency—to accept or reject the actions of an otherwise technically proficient performer in producing sound. Through the phrasing of "people say," he was able to argue that the horse fiddle has its own will without the social risk of claiming that the fiddle is alive. In other words, because he was reporting on an aspect of cultural heritage, he could make ontological claims that are incompatible with neoliberal modernity without positioning himself outside of modernity.

Modernities

In the twentieth century, Mongolia underwent two waves of modernization resulting from two different global colonial movements from the west. The first was the Soviet modernization project, based on the Leninist formulation of a state-run industrial economy and a Tylorian ideal of a populace free of superstition. In the early 1990s, Mongolia, like the rest of the postsocialist world, was remodernized through strict demands from international monetary institutions to dismantle social services and adopt stringent neoliberal reforms in order to qualify for subsidies to rebuild their economy after the collapse of the Soviet Union, a process known as "neoliberal shock therapy" (Buyandelger 2013). These two visions of modernity share certain foundational ideals—secularism, progress, and industrialization of the economy. However, they differ in fundamental ways, especially concerning the open expression of "spiritual" ideas.

The first modernization campaign was the imposition of Soviet power, economy, and ideology that came from Mongolia's induction as the first satellite state of the USSR (Isono 1976). Though it was never officially a colony of the Soviet Union, and it joined the Soviet cause to escape a previous colonization by the Qing Empire, the People's Republic of Mongolia was nonetheless subjected to Soviet modernization campaigns under considerable pressure from Moscow (Bawden 1989; Sneath 2003; Buyandelger 2013). The Mongolian People's Revolutionary Party took control of the country with a military that was trained, armed, and supported by the Soviet Red Army and ruled with the explicit knowledge that Mongolia's independence from the Qing Empire (and later, China) was dependent on maintaining its status as a "Little Brother" to the USSR (Sneath 2003).

At the beginning of the twentieth century, the ruling party of the People's Republic of Mongolia considered the persisting political authority held by the Buddhist establishment to be the primary hindrance for establishing a socialist state (Kaplonski 2014). As such, party members treated the secularization of the country as a precondition for the production of a modern socialist Mongolia. By 1939 the Mongolian People's Army, under direction from Marshal Choibalsan, had forcibly closed almost all the monasteries and defrocked most of the monks in Mongolia, leading functionally to the temporary end of organized religion in the country (Bawden 1989, 348).

Traditional music played a major role in socialist modernization. I will discuss the institutionalization of traditional music in the twentieth century in more detail in chapter 2. At this stage, it is important to point out that the secularization of the music itself was a part of its incorporation into the socialist project. The horse fiddle in its current form was adapted, standardized, and mobilized by representatives of the socialist state and allies from the Soviet Union during the twentieth century to symbolize the modern, cosmopolitan, socialist Mongolian nation (Marsh 2009). Long-song underwent similar adaptations during this period. In chapter 6, I will describe one such case, in which representatives from the state called in a long-song singer to edit her song by removing most of the language and symbolism referring to Buddhism before she was allowed to record the song for radio play.

The second modernization was the neoliberal transformation that came with the transition from single-party socialist state to parliamentary democracy. International monetary organizations designed neoliberal shock therapy to integrate nascent postsocialist postcolonies into global capitalism by requiring those countries to defund and privatize public services and resources to qualify for aid (Verdery 1996). During the post-socialist restructuring of Mongolia, the majority of political parties (Zul and Cheng 2022) and citizens alike (Shagdar 2007) were not in favor of creating a neoliberal "free market" initially. However, as politicians operating under political pressure from the United States looked internationally for financial support to rebuild the country's economy from scratch, they turned to the International Monetary Fund (IMF) and the Asian Development ment Bank for loans (Zul and Cheng 2022). The government rolled out neoliberal policies without much information made available to the public and with little public support (Shagdar 2007).

Neoliberal shock therapy rapidly underdeveloped Mongolia throughout the 1990s. Sneath (2003) argues that within global geopolitics Mongolia is functionally in a similar position to a postcolony. As such, in the neoliberal era the country is subject to neocolonialism in which more powerful states exercise control over the country through political and economic pressure (Nkrumah 1976). Most prominently in Mongolia, this neocolonialism takes the form of mineral exploitation by Western mining corporations with un-equal contracts. The country also experiences exploitative political pres-sure from Russia, China, and United States to build natural gas pipelines, provide material and land for the Belt and Road Project, and send citizens to participate in the United States' wars in the Middle East, respectively.

The transition to capitalist democracy led to a renewed freedom of reli-gious practice (Pedersen 2011; Wallace 2012; Buyandelger 2013). However, the neoliberalization of society resulted in other forms of disconnection from spirituality. Capitalism is, simply put, disenchanting (Weber 1955; Weber, Roth, and Wittich 1978). After the transition, individualism became a more prominent value in Mongolia as the country entered the global capitalist market. Proponents of neoliberalism, like the IMF, push people to internalize the core values of individualism and personal responsibility in order to diminish social networks among the working class (Harvey 2005). Though practicing religion in public is no longer banned and many monasteries have reopened, neoliberal ideology nevertheless exerts pressure to individualize as many aspects of social life as possible. In the same way that the alienating drive of capitalism isolates people from one another and from ecological networks of relation with nonhuman animals, plants, and fungi (Tsing 2015), it also separates people from supernatural networks of relation as well (Bubandt 2017; Fernando 2022).

The socialist era involved the disentanglement of spirits from social life in obvious ways. The Soviet-inspired ban on public religious practice pushed people to either abandon spiritual practice, recontextualize their beliefs through the epistemology of colonial secularism, or practice in secret. As the ban on religion softened throughout the 1980s and was eventually discarded as part of Mongolia's turn toward parliamentary democracy in the early 1990s, the practice of religion emerged back into public life in the country. However, a resurgence in religious practice is not the same as a reentanglement of nonsecular entities into ecological thinking at the institutional and state levels.

One of the foundational assertions of the post-Enlightenment thought that led to both socialist and neoliberal modernity is the separation of "nature" from "culture" (Strathern 1980; Descola and Sahlins 2014). Wrapped up in this disentanglement of human from nature was the separation of the human and the supernatural as well. Modernity, whether socialist or capitalist, depends on a particular European political ideology of secularization concerned with the isolation of religion into its own discrete social realm, which both extracts spiritual practices from other aspects of society and lessens its social effect (Asad 2003; Casanova 2009). In Mongolia, where traditional religions involve a deep entanglement of spiritual practice and land-based energies (Humphrey 1995), these two disentanglements, human from nature and human from supernature, are connected and reinforce one another (Madison Pískatá 2018).

When people in contemporary Mongolia engage with the spiritual entities in their more-than-human networks of social relation, it is often in counter-hegemonic ways. In his study of the eruption of shamanic spirits in northern Mongolia after the transition to postsocialism, Pedersen (2011) argues that young Darhad men engage with (and are engaged by) these spirits as a response to the disintegration of the economy and the dissolution of social networks that came with neoliberal reform. Buyandelger (2013), also writing on shamanism, contends that in the postsocialist era, Buryat shamans have started to build relationships with the spirits of ancestors to put together a counter-hegemonic historiography of their community in direct conflict with the official narratives of the state. In her work on Buddhism, Wallace (2012) finds that Mongolian practitioners are faced with a "crisis of modernity" as they navigate the legacies of Soviet-style anti-religious modernity alongside the emergent difficulties that the individualism and materialism of capitalist modernity present to religious practice (90). Horse fiddle players navigate these same structures. Ideological holdovers from the high Soviet secularism of the socialist era permeate the institutions where they learn, teach, and perform the instrument. The alienating drive of capitalism strains their ability to build and maintain more-than-human networks of relation.

The Soviet project established musical institutions to bring about modernity and enforce modern forms of power (a process I will cover in more detail in chapter 2). Later on, neoliberal shock therapy demanded significant cuts to the funding for all public institutions, conservatories included. Despite these cuts, institutions set up in the Soviet model, like the National Conservatory, continue to be at the center of music education. Significantly, these institutions now house the mechanisms for applying for cultural heritage status with UNESCO, bringing socialist-era structures into global, neoliberal institutions.

Siloing cultural resources into state-run projects and then cutting their funding streams is not deinstitutionalization so much as the development of institutions with high social power and low financial capacity. Nor does this state of affairs represent the removal of politics from the economy of music. Rather, the case of the post-Soviet, postcolonial conservatory highlights a disjuncture between the persisting socialist-era organization of local institutions and the global imposition of neoliberal politics that are unable to sustainably support music and heritage.

In spaces like the conservatory, the incongruity between neoliberalism and the enduring, material legacies of socialism create problems that are impossible to reconcile with modern solutions. Examples of these problems crop up throughout this book. In chapter 2, fiddle teachers deal with a lack of resources to teach the music to their satisfaction. Later on in chapter 5, artists struggle with the issue of being unable to support themselves through music. However, the disjuncture between the two modernities also allows for opportunities to fold alterity into the institution. As musicians turn to nonsecular, more-than-human networks to navigate these problems, they create spaces for imagining and working toward nonsecular, more-than-human futures.

The overarching mission of modernity is the homogenization and rationalization of society (Harvey 1989). The People's Revolutionary Party sought to create an undifferentiated field of socialist citizens, while under neoliberal modernity both heads of state and heads of industry aim to transform all humans into ideal consumers. However, as Lisa Rofel (1999) argues, modernity takes different forms according to local desires. For Trouillot (2003) modernization is a project designed to re-create the West on a global scale and it depends on the creation of a native "others" to compare against. Colonial powers devised "alter-natives," other modernities that exist alongside and in opposition to the global colonial modernity of the West, to justify oppression and exploitation (Trouillot 2003). However, the inhabitants of those alternative modernities are aware of their position relative to colonizing powers. Furthermore, they have the capacity to create and pursue their own desires that act in opposition to hegemonic global frameworks. For Mongolian musicians navigating postsocialism, this means driving wind-horses through the cracks left by neoliberal and socialist modernity crashing into one another.

The Wind that Moves the Hand of the Fiddler

When I first asked the horse fiddle teacher and performer Ganbold about the relationships between the fiddle and animals, he told me that music was a useful tool for calming down livestock. He went on to explain that the fiddle is primarily for horses and camels, while singing is appropriate for sheep, goats, and cattle. In Ganbold's breakdown, this division relates to how close or far away different animals are pastured from the encampment. Sheep, goats, and cattle are typically kept close to home in Mongolian pastoralist encampments and are therefore easier to calm. Camels and horses, on the other hand, are pastured far from the encampment and develop strong wills while away from their herders. The horse fiddle has the special power to calm these semi-independent livestock.

Ganbold's breakdown of the inner worlds of different livestock animals included different overall emotional characters. For horses, which Ganbold described as nervous and independent, the fiddle calms them and makes them docile. Meanwhile, the fiddle causes camels, sentimental and dramatic creatures, to weep. As I will describe in chapter 3, I saw firsthand how dramatic camels could be—prone to antics and wailing into the night sky.

In this formulation, the power of the fiddle derives from folk religion, situated in subsistence mobile pastoralism. The ideal performance of the horse fiddle as he described it would find the fiddler in a *ger*, the felt round-tent dwelling used by nomadic herders. In the circular space of the *ger*, the sound can travel upward, spiraling out through the roof ring, which holds the top of the tent in place. The sound then travels out and hits the ear of the horses. The tune should then calm the horses and make them docile, especially if it is an *uyangyn urtyn duu*, a "melodious long-song."

Ganbold then moved on to explain that for camels, if you have access to a horse fiddle but no fiddler, you can put a fiddle on the animal's humps and face it toward the wind. The air moving along the strings will cause the fiddle to resound, which in turn will calm the camel. Camels are tall enough that their humps catch strong and consistent wind coming off the steppe. The wind plays the fiddle. "People say," Ganbold added, using the phrasing of communal wisdom I described above, "that the *süns* of the fiddle is like a wind that guides the hand of a fiddler, just like how I guide the hand of my students when they are first starting to play the instrument."

In this explanation, Ganbold used the *ger* as a metaphor for Mongolian nomadic pastoralism. Ganbold argued that the horse fiddle has maintained this spiritual relationship with horses and camels as well as its importance to folk religious ritual because it never left the space of the *ger*. For him, the horse fiddle did not become a court instrument like the *shanz* (lute) and was never fully made into a classical instrument enough to be divorced from the *ger*.

I have known Ganbold since 2010, as a friend and as a research contact. Throughout countless conversations and interviews over the years, I have heard him become more self-consciously spiritual in his perspectives on the fiddle. When I first returned to Mongolia in 2016, he told me in an interview that he had had a spiritual awakening while performing atop a sacred boulder at Khamaryn Khiid, a monastery adjoining a holistic energy healing center in the eastern Gobi province of Dornogovi. That he would tie his spiritual awakening to a place where Buddhism and New Age flow together is indicative of the larger picture of the kinds of spiritual hybridity unfolding in Mongolia at the moment. He is a Buddhist and calls on monks to perform rites. He also follows New Age beliefs about manifesting events into being. As for the *süns* of the horse fiddle, he takes a shamanic perspective and describes the *süns* as a kind of soul.

This soul, the spirit giving a human life, should not be confused with a Christian soul. As Ganbold explained, a person can have many. In his words,

> Everyone has their own *süns*, you have yours and I have mine, but in each of us there may be more than one. You could be holding on to your great-great-great-great-whatever, some ancestor's *süns* too. If a person is angry all the time, it is because they have a *süns* on high that is filling them with anger. That is why a soul must be guided out of a body when someone has passed away and guided on the right path. Otherwise they will hang around and instill grief and emotional distress on their family and neighbors. For this you need someone much like a musician . . . a monk!

There are two notable takeaways from this quote. The first is that, though he cloaks this claim in humor, Ganbold draws a clear comparison between the power of horse fiddle players and Buddhist monks. Both are religious specialists in his explanation, with the ability to guide spirits in a similar manner. The second important takeaway from this quote is that, in Ganbold's construction, each fiddler has at least one soul. Horses also have souls, though he did not mention whether other nonhuman animals do or not. This *süns* that the fiddle gives moves the fiddler's hand.

Ganbold makes the explicit claim that not only does the fiddle have its own *süns*, but that furthermore it is *am'd*, alive. The fiddle has a *süns* and is alive because it is constructed of living elements. The fiddle is made with hair from the living horse, never a dead one. Through this hair, the fiddle has a connection with that horse and its *süns*. The human performer then imbues the instrument with their own *süns* by playing it. The performance bonds the fiddle and the fiddler to that horse's soul.

Ganbold explained that in his view, the confluence of the human musician's *süns* with that of the horse via the sympathetic connection formed by the instrument's body creates a separate soul for the fiddle. He used metaphors from shamanism to make this argument, likening the performance of the fiddle to the meeting of winds coming from the east and west. In Mongolian shamanic cosmology, the winds of the east and the winds of the west are the physical manifestations of two competing groups of *tengri*, spiritual beings residing from the heavens who created the first humans (Khangalov 1890, 363–64). Though western *tengri* are often considered benevolent to humans and eastern *tengri* malevolent, shamans derive their spiritual and social power by entreating both. When the two winds meet, they create a third that travels its own direction, without losing any part of their original trajectories.

Ganbold added, "There is a thick string and a thin string on the fiddle, but when you play together you get a third sound—a sound that is at once both of the others and a sound unique to itself." The soul of the human and of the horse makes a third soul for the fiddle. By playing, you develop the insight to see beyond the two, and in so doing make visible another dimension of both. Ganbold finished this explication with an appeal to restorative nostalgia: "We once knew all about this, then we forgot. Now we are just remembering it again."

Ganbold's description of the soul of a person, a horse, and a musical instrument is a radical break with post-Enlightenment rational division of humans, nature, and human-produced objects. He has developed this worldview throughout his career as a horse fiddler, slowly moving from a secular way of conceptualizing the instrument to this elaborated understanding that positions the fiddle as an *am'd* ("living") object, the mediates the relationship between a human performer and a horse. He consistently tied this spiritual perspective to elements of cultural heritage, situating the horse fiddle in the larger frame of nomadic pastoralist tradition.

Buddha and Erlig Khan

Ganbold's explanation above focuses on the role of horse fiddle music in connecting humans with nonhuman animals. However, horse fiddle music, and long-song in particular, are also useful tools for connecting humans with nonliving nonhumans, especially mountains. As I will explore in more detail in chapter 5, Tüvshee, the fiddler from the University of Arts and Culture, reported that he performs the horse fiddle for sacred mountains as a form of religious practice. He referred to this kind of performance as a fundamental aspect of practicing his Buddhism. Buddhism is Mongolia's most practiced religion, both before and after the transition.

Tüvshee offered that the wood used in the construction of the fiddle's body and the tree sap used as rosin are key to the fiddler's ability to produce music that resonates with humans, horses, and the land alike. While Ganbold's reading was more animistic, Tüvshee attributed the fiddle's potential to reach not only nonhuman animals, but nonliving nonhumans as well, to the unifying power of Buddha.

His explanation took the form of a religious folktale: "To tell you this story I should introduce you to two characters: the Buddha and the Erlig Khan. Buddha works tirelessly to help the beings of the world to elevate themselves in life from his palace in the sky. Erlig Khan, the god of death in Black Shamanism, lives in the earth." From the very beginning, this story entangles Buddhism with other forms of Mongolian spirituality, invoking a shared deity, the Erlig Khan, between the Mongolian form of Tibetan Buddhism and Black Shamanism, the branch of shamanism dedicated to preventing harm by entreating dangerous spirits.

Tüvshee continued with the tale, telling of how the Erlig Khan sent one of his attendants to spy on Buddha. The attendant found Buddha working on a project to bring joy to humankind. He took some hair from the mane and tail of his most beloved horse and fashioned the first horse fiddle. When he bowed the fiddle, however, its sound was awful. It was scratchy, quiet, and thin.

The attendant returned to Erlig Khan with this news. After some consideration, Erlig Khan said, "Take him sap from our black tree and have him rub it on the bow and strings." When the attendant returned, he gave the rosin according to Erlig Khan's instruction. The fiddle resounded brilliantly, with a deep and moving tone.

The point of the story, Tüvshee told me, is that the horse fiddle is itself a religious artifact. The human performer, the heavenly horsehair of its strings, and the earthly wood and sap used in its construction and performance connect all beings. Like Ganbold, Tüvshee brought up that the fiddle has two strings, which you play together to create a melody. He said to play the horse fiddle is to know that you must have life along with death, joy along with sorrow, in order to have beauty in this world. The fiddle is made from the living elements of beings from the sky and from the earth. In the middle, the fiddler imbues it with a human spirit in performance. That is why the instrument can connect humans with the other beings in creation. The *süns* in this sense is a natural spirit that is creation of the Buddha working in tandem with the Erlig Khan.

Though Tüvshee's performance of horse fiddle for sacred mountains is a personal, private ritual that he conducts alone, I found in other interviews that he is not alone in practicing his religion this way. Another fiddler, whom I will call Baatar, mentioned that he also plays horse fiddle as a kind lay Buddhist rite, but he pointed out that spiritual practices associated with the horse fiddle tend to be hybrid by nature.

Like Ganbold, Baatar described the horse fiddle as "alive." Baatar argued that the ability to sound nonhumans gave the instrument spiritual power. "When I play for a sacred mountain," he explained, "I choose a song that channels water, wind, and wild animals. I sound the entire environment of the mountain and thus becomes a ritual of praise for it."

Baatar explained that the horse fiddle's *süns* is central to the hybridity between lay Buddhist practice, shamanism, and other folk religious practice in Mongolia. The fiddle has power as a Buddhist tool, a folk religious tool, a shamanic tool, and a herding tool because its *süns* gives human performers access to a more-than-human frame of knowledge. As he put it, the music of the fiddle "does not bring the sky to us, but us to the sky. Its spirit is not inherently Buddhist, not nomadic, nor shamanic. It is perhaps Mongol, but most importantly it is a horse. A horse does not belong to its destination, but it ferries the rider there."

Vibrations

After having heard the term *sünstei khögjim* in several interviews, I decided to ask Tuyaa, one of the musicologists at the National Conservatory, how she would describe the term. She did not like the term *sünstei khögjim* ("instrument with a spirit") and offered instead *sünsleg avia* ("spiritual sound"). She told me that the *süns* is a metaphor; it simply means the fiddle can touch the hearts of Mongolian people and furthermore has the ability to pull the talent out of a performer.

Throughout the interview, Tuyaa's answers started to take on more of an enchanted tone. She told me that "the strings are from a living horse, and the bow is also made from living horsehair. That's why when the bow hits the strings, the sound is so touching." The importance of the living elements used in the fiddle's construction is one of the constants running throughout my interviews. She continued, "From a young age I always knew this instrument had a *süns*, had flesh and blood, I just didn't know how to put it into words. Now I can say the word for it is *energi*. That is the character of the fiddle, its quality. The *energi* of the fiddle is the instrument's wind and breath."

Though she distanced herself from overtly Buddhist or shamanic readings of this force, she did refer to the fiddle's power using a spiritual term, *energi*. Though derived from the Russian *energi*, a cognate with the English word "energy," in the Mongolian usage, *energi* (pronounced "enerik") has a particular spiritual meaning. Madison Pískatá (2021a) describes *energi* as a form of energy in a distinctly Mongolian style of New Age spirituality. *Energi* in her formulation is a postsocialist reinterpretation of what Humphrey (1995) refers to as "energies-in-nature," earth-based sources of power in the Mongolian tradition. People in Mongolia draw upon this concept of *energi* to explain social relationships with geological bodies that are not alive but are "lively" (Madison Pískatá 2024). *Energi*, as Madison Pískatá argues, demonstrates that New Age thought, as neither fully religious nor actually secular, flourishes in postsocialist contexts with a histories of religious repression.

"New Age" is a slippery term, as it is not an organized religion so much as a loose collection of ideas and practices. By New Age in this case, I am particularly interested in what Hanegraaff (1998) refers to as ideologies that sacralize psychology and psychologize religion. New Age uses the secular, modernist rhetoric of pseudoscience to allow enchantment to operate within a modernist, rationalist mode. Folkways that were repressed as "superstition" under the socialist model, like using stones for their healing properties, find a new life in neoliberalism as New Age practices through the language of science and pseudoscience.

I have noticed New Age ideas become more prevalent in Mongolia since 2010, especially, but not exclusively, among middle-aged people who grew up in the secular state and experienced the transition to religious freedom as adults. The horse fiddle is a magnet for New Age, given its role as a ritual tool in Mongolian folk culture. For example, I have heard several New Age explanations related to the custom of playing fiddle for housewarming parties and Lunar New Year celebrations.

In both Ulaanbaatar and the rural county where I do research in Dund-govi, people know me as a horse fiddle player. This home cleansing ritual, known as *javar ürgeekh* (literally "to lift the chill") is a common aspect of being a fiddle player and as such I have been called to perform it many times. The novelty of my position as a foreigner playing this instrument and dutifully carrying out the social obligations of a fiddler comes with social testing; at each performance I have been grilled on what the ritual really means. While I usually give the same reply, "the ritual is about clear-ing bad spirits out of a house," the corrections I have received tend to lean on New Age concepts.

One middle-aged man told me, "*Javar* is not a spirit, like a ghost or something. It is negative sentiments that settle into a place. So, you are not lifting out bad spirits, just bad feelings that make you feel upset." One woman, whom I will refer to as Pagmaa, drew a more direct connection between the ritual and New Age, arguing that *javar ürgeekh* is a form of manifestation, using the vibrations of the fiddle to drive away negative ideas and instill positive outcomes. She went on to argue that Mongolian folk religion is a precursor to New Age thought. Referring to the New Age self-help bestseller, *The Secret*, Pagmaa said, "Really, Mongolians have known the secret for a long time."

For Tuyaa, the *süns* of the horse fiddle is *energi*. *Energi* has a physical manifestation as the vibrations that the fiddle produces. These vibrations align with the hearts of their audiences, human and nonhuman alike. Further, she argued that *energi* guides the hand of the fiddler, mirroring Ganbold's claims above.

As in the previous examples, Tuyaa's answer involves hybridity with folk religion and Buddhism. The Energiin Töv ("energy center") at Khamariin Khiid Monastery in Dornogovi province, where Ganbold had his spiritual awakening, is a pilgrimage site that brings together Buddhist and New Age rituals. It draws Buddhist power from the lineage of the Gobi saint Danzanravjaa, and its *energi* from the field of volcanic rock upon which the monastery is built.

Conclusion

In each of these three explanations, a performer's ability to connect with the spirits, energies, or vibrations of landscape and livestock places the horse fiddle as a mediator between humans and nonhumans. The fiddle's spirit has its own kind of agency that extends into both human and ungulate worlds, whether as a wind which guides the hand of the fiddler, a Buddhist incantation which bestows protection and guidance upon them, or as a conduit for energy which draws out their hidden potential.

The multiplicity of explanations and interpretations of the horse fiddle's spirit gestures to an important facet of postsocialist Mongolian life: an unfolding pluralistic spiritual awakening that at times defies official narratives and capitalist categorization. Each of the explanations for the *süns* of the fiddle represents a potential more-than-human future. The networks of relation that each explanation connects to the correct performance of the horse fiddle tie together humans, nonhuman animals, and other entities in configurations that are otherwise incompatible with the institutions where they teach and play their instruments. In the following chapter, I will delve further into the institutionalization of horse fiddle music and the ways fiddlers bring nonhumans into these institutions.

When I first started working with musicians in the region in 2010, many people were still very tentative about speaking publicly on religious or spiritual practices and beliefs. Many fiddlers I work with have told me that since I first met them, they have come to realize that spirits have more power than they originally thought and have changed their approach to the fiddle accordingly. In this way, reflections on nonhumans' ability to consume horse fiddle music open up discourses on postsocialist personhood and spirituality. Cultural heritage creates the discursive space for people to be able to critically examine the world and their relationships with nonhumans without having to leave the ontological confines of modernity.

CHAPTER 2

THE MELODIOUS
HOOFBEAT

September 21 of 2017 marked the first day of rehearsal for the newly formed Morin Khuuryn Nairuulga, or Horse Fiddle Symphony, and the first snow of the year. This snow was a little early, but not unseasonably so for Ulaanbaatar. On my walk to the Students' Theater at the Arts and Culture University, the snow left icy stings on my face and pools of water on the sidewalk. In a few months, winter would be marked not by snow, but by the descent of air pollution, as coal dust from home heating would become trapped in the city's inversion layer. On the first day of rehearsals I did not yet need an N95 mask, a sign that winter was still far off.

A few weeks earlier I had met with Pürevkhüü, the chair of the horse fiddle department. He agreed to assist with my research, offering me opportunities to participate in department activities. In exchange, he asked that I participate in a new project he was organizing—the Horse Fiddle Symphony. I was to join the orchestra with my own fiddle and in exchange I could interview professors in his department, himself included. By the end of September, I already had a few interviews under my belt and the time had come to make good on my side of the deal.

Pürevkhüü explained that this orchestra was brand new, the result of an agreement between the Arts and Culture University and a nongovernmental organization called the Morin Khuuryn Töv (Morin Khuur Center). Their goal as to establish what Pürevkhüü referred to as "not just an ensemble, but a full orchestra of horse fiddle and Mongolian instruments. Well," he continued in his characteristic joking fashion, "all Mongolian instruments plus a piano."

When I arrived at the Students' Theater for the first rehearsal, I saw that most of the other performers had already arrived and set up in formations. On the right side of the stage sat thirty or so fiddlers. Across from them were ten more along with two standing performers with *ikh khuur*, essentially the horse fiddle equivalent to an upright bass with two thick, steel strings instead of horsehair bundles. Between the two sections were a handful of *yatga* (zither) players. I told Pürevkhüü that I was not a very good performer, but he just grinned and told me that did not matter. He directed me to join the *ayalguu*, or melody section, on the right half of the stage. I could not find a seat, and went over to the left instead, to be with the *khooloi*, or harmony, section.

The performers were all students at the university, mostly seniors and juniors, with a couple of sophomores and freshmen and one master's student joining in. After I settled in, Pürevkhüü came over and told me, "Ours is a truly international orchestra." He pointed out several students from Inner Mongolia and a few from Buryatia in Russia. "And now we have an American!" he laughed.

We practiced two songs throughout the evening, "Romans" ("Romance") by Altankhuyag and Pürevkhüü's own "Ikeliin Egshigt Nutag" ("Homeland with the Melody of the *Ikel*"). "Romans" is a conventional, neo-romantic composition. "Ikeliin Egshigt Nutag," on the other hand, draws heavily on *tatlagan-ayaz*, a genre of traditional music that calls on the performer to acoustically mimic various gaits of different kinds of horses. *Tatlagan-ayaz* was the style of song that Dad'süren played at the Gobi *nair*. As part of their education at the conservatories of Ulaanbaatar, the fiddle students in this orchestra were expected to be proficient at *tatlagan-ayaz* and *tatlagan-ayaz*-inflected classical pieces like this one.

My single, strongest memory of that first rehearsal was how cold my feet were. About halfway through the evening several students had started to pull on jackets. By the end of practice almost everyone was fiddling in their overcoats. While the first chair took a solo, my stand partner mimed shivering and said, in English, "Cold."

Ulaanbaatar is the coldest capital city of any country in the world. Winter temperatures often reach –40 degrees, the point at which Fahrenheit and Celsius overlap. Despite the extremes of midwinter, the coldest part of the year, to me, is the last two weeks of September.

As a remnant of the Soviet style of central heating, all the radiators in offices, businesses, schools, and apartment buildings throughout the city turn on no earlier than October 1. Once the heat is on, there is no turning it off until the shutoff date of May 1. This cycle of centralized heating is a socialist rhythm and a colonial rhythm. The heat turns on and off in a cycle that tracks the seasons according to when cold weather is likely to start in Europe, not in Mongolia. The night of the first rehearsal, the temperature fell to the low 30s Fahrenheit. The night of the following rehearsal, it fell into the mid-teens. This cycle, adopted from the Soviet Union, flouts the natural rhythm of the changing seasons.

Walking back home through the mid-autumn snow that evening, I was stuck on the image of all of us in the orchestra, in that post-Soviet concert hall. There we were, shivering in Canada Goose jackets, trying to evoke the sounds of a summertime horse pasture. I wondered about these twenty-something-year-olds, many of whom had spent their entire lives up to this point ensconced in a physically and mentally demanding conservatory track. My stand partner had said that he started his training at age five, and everyone else in my section had started before reaching sixteen. How were these fiddlers, learning from institutions in the capital city, meant to learn how to play a song like a horse runs?

Rhythm and the Institution

Tatlagan-ayaz, also commonly known by the shorter name *tatlaga*, is a genre of quick, rhythmic, lyric-less horse fiddle tunes that often evoke the different gaits of horses, camels, and bulls. The horse fiddlers I worked with all described the process of learning a *tatlagan-ayaz* as beginning with careful observation of the moods and movements of livestock animals as they move through pastures over the course of a season. A successful performance of *tatlagan-ayaz* depends on the player's ability to embody the animal portrayed in the song through their fiddling. For urban-based, professional horse fiddle players, success on their instrument requires them to be able to bring the disparate rhythms of the institution and the pasture into eurhythmia, a sublime state in which concordance between rhythms allows for the performer to create a piece of art that is greater than the sum of its parts (Lefebvre 2004).

The multispecies nature of this genre chafes at the rationalizing edges of the colonial modernist project. In Mongolia, this disjuncture is further complicated by the fact that colonial modernist projects have been enacted twice. During the socialist period, it was not uncommon for horse fiddle performers to travel to rural pastures to supplement their conservatory education with deeper understanding of the rhythms of livestock animals, reshaping the flows of knowledge and warping the unidirectional flow from center to periphery in the process. Now, thirty years into postsocialist capitalist democracy, horse fiddle teachers are faced with the prospect that addressing the same problem of how to incorporate horses, camels, and bulls into urban music education will require new solutions.

Institutions like the Arts and Culture University have rhythms. From the everyday rhythm of classes beginning and ending, to the pseudo-seasonal rhythms of the fall and spring semesters, to the grand rhythms of classes entering and graduating. Institutional rhythms are made up of the people passing through, from large-scale movements right down to the minute rhythms of the body (Lefebvre 2004). What horse fiddlers realize is that not all of these bodies are necessarily human. Focusing on the rhythms of bodily practice allows for a multispecies approach to understanding music that does not require estimates or assertions on the mental inner worlds of nonhumans.

Reentangling heritage with nonhumans requires fiddlers to flex and bend the otherwise rigid temporalities of music institutions. Nonhumans have their own rhythms that are not always in sync with the institution. For these performers to use cultural heritage in a way that can persist under a neoliberal model while maintaining the potential to imagine outside of neoliberalism, they must navigate both.

In this chapter, I present the opinions and educational strategies of horse fiddle teachers based out of conservatories and orchestras in Ulaanbaatar that were either originally formed during the socialist period or operate under the socialist-era institutional model, particularly the National Conservatory (formerly the Music and Dance College), the University of Arts and Culture's Department of Music, and the National Philharmonic's

State Horse Fiddle Ensemble. I draw heavily on the oral histories and peda-gogical strategies of music teachers like Ganbold and Ganaa, both of whom are horse fiddle players based out of Ulaanbaatar who attribute much of their success with the instrument to knowing how to learn rhythms from livestock animals and how to translate those rhythms to the fiddle. I bring in perspectives from several members of an informal group of concerned horse fiddle teachers based out of these institutions, including Bilgüün, Ganaa, and Erdene, all of whom are middle-aged men who live in Ulaan-baatar for part of the year and spend part of the year (the midwinter and summer months) in various rural locales.

The central role that rural, nonhuman animals perform in the trans-mission of *tatlagan-ayaz* pushes fiddlers to explore the limits of modernist institutions. Ganbold, Ganaa, and Erdene recall their own formative years learning *tatlagan-ayaz* in the socialist era when they had opportunities to engage with horses, bulls, and camels in their pastures. The performers I worked with fondly recalled breaking the institutional rhythm of reporting to the conservatory in Ulaanbaatar each day by taking long stays in rural encampments. However, when teachers attempt to provide those same educational experiences to their students now, they find themselves flum-moxed by incompatibilities between the socialist model and postsocialist conditions of their conservatories.

Pursuit of pastoral rhythms in both cases are described as disruptions to the regular schedule of musical institutions. However, horse fiddle students are encouraged to find moments to step away from the official rhythm of classical music education, to leave the conservatory for rural pastures, in order to improve their mastery over *tatlagan-ayaz*. Horse fid-dlers are expected to develop the ability to sound the conservatory during classical performance and sound difference from the conservatory during performance of heritage music.

Students who break the institutional rhythm rarely break from the institutions themselves. To the contrary, being able to convincingly play in such a way that evokes pastoral rhythms is something that the director of the National Horse Fiddle Ensemble told me he looks for when audi-tioning perspective performers. As fiddlers take breaks from institutional rhythm to pursue parallel music education in the pastures, they strengthen the cultural hegemony of the institution by subsuming rural, more-than-human approaches to the transmission and performance of heritage into the institutional model. However, through these breakages fiddlers also undermine the modernist institution's core assumption of separating nature from culture by transforming the spatial-temporal rhythm of conservatory education according to the material needs of nonhuman animals.

Rhythm in *Tatlagan-ayaz*

In my first interview with Ganbold, a horse fiddle teacher and *tatlagan-ayaz* specialist, he told me that he has two distinct pedagogical approaches to the instrument. He said, "For classical music, for jazz and the like, you can learn from sheet music, but for *tatlagan-ayaz*, you need to learn from livestock." A member of the National Philharmonic, whom I will refer here to as Ganaa, supported Ganbold's position, saying, "A teacher can give you the general shape of a particular *tatlagan-ayaz* tune, but to really play the song you need the horse." Both Ganbold and Ganaa explained that you need livestock to be able to learn this genre because the songs' time signatures resist standardization.

Ganaa argued that you can hear the difference between a fiddler who counts time as a classical musician and a fiddler who counts time in a livestock-educated way. He told me, "Consider the famous Gobi fiddler Nergüi Khuurch. When he plays you can tell he isn't counting time. He keeps his own time, a time based on pulses." This pulse time, he explained, draws from livestock gaits, translating the different movements of horses, camels, and bulls into discernible rhythms.

"In music school," Ganaa continued, "you are taught to count time. A song can be 3/4 or 4/4, and so on, but the rural *tatlagan-ayaz* style does not use those time signatures well." Great *tatlaga*, according to Ganaa, is best performed according to a personal, individual keeping of time that draws from the performer's relationship with a particular animal. Though standard pedagogy at conservatories teaches fiddlers to keep an unchanging time signature throughout the course of a given piece and to reproduce that structure over multiple performances, teachers like Ganaa and Ganbold pointed out that performing *tatlagan-ayaz* in this way sounds off.

For Ganaa, Ganbold, and many of the other teachers I interviewed, *tatlagan-ayaz* involves a careful observation of the various rhythms of nonhuman animals. Tomie Hahn (2007) writes that the process of learning dance involves "kinesthetic synesthesia," an overlapping of the senses in which the student transforms what they see into the feelings of bodily movement needed to carry out the performance. The fiddlers I worked with described a similar process, but at the multispecies level. To learn *tatlagan-ayaz*, Ganaa, Ganbold, and Bilgüün all explained that they watched horses, camels, and bulls and translated their visual interpretation of those animals' movements into the bodily sensation needed to capture a song's rhythm.

A horse does not always keep a steady beat. It changes speeds and gaits, stops to turn, kick, and play. A camel will bellow, trundle, and preen as it takes to the steppe in the morning. A bull might charge forward, but suddenly stop short and paw at the earth. A good fiddler should be able to extrapolate a wide range of rhythms from the social life of the horse, camel, or bull over the course of a song. Performances that stick too rigidly to a given time signature take nonhuman animals as objects to be mimicked. Ganaa says these performances lack feeling. Ideally, *tatlagan-ayaz* takes the livestock as subjects and interprets their gaits and behaviors through the horse fiddle in ways that should theoretically appeal to both humans and horses alike.

Socialist-Era Memories

Throughout the twentieth century, Mongolia's People's Revolutionary Party, like many other socialist governments of the time, used state-approved folk music as a key cultural tool for building public confidence in the socialist nation and implementing ideological goals of the socialist project (Marsh 2009). The "cultural work," or the mobilization of arts, ritual practice, and tradition in the legitimation of state power and the production of proper socialist citizens throughout the twentieth century (Bloch 2004; Marsh 2009), has had a lasting effect on people's lives across the postsocialist world. Throughout the Soviet Union, "Houses of Culture" were established to be the center of social life, hosting holiday celebrations and artistic and sports clubs that continue to play a role in the daily social lives of citizens after the collapse of the Soviet Union. State authorities elevated historically regional, small-scale musical practices to the level of national music, standardizing the performance aesthetics and pedagogy and establishing a number of state folk orchestras (Rice 1996; Bulag 1998; Buchanan 2006; Marsh 2009).

To create a new workforce of professional folk musicians, socialist states institutionalized the transmission of music, adapting pedagogies to replace presocialist informal or nonstandardized contexts of music education with state conservatories. The Mongolian state established conservatories that adapted European classical music notation and pedagogical forms to presocialist styles of music and musical instruments that had previously been taught and learned through nonstandardized aural-visual-tactile processes to prepare musicians to play in state classical and folk orchestras (Marsh 2009). In Mongolia (Pegg 2001), as in other Soviet satellites like Bulgaria (Rice 1996), institutionalizing traditional instrument education involved transitioning from a mimicry-based teaching style to the use of notated sheet music as part of the separation of institutional music learning from rural practice.

For Mongolian horse fiddle performers, this led to two distinct rhythms of music education. To become professional musicians, fiddlers would move to an urban center and appear at the conservatory to run drills during work hours on weekdays, and for half the day on Saturdays. Proficiency in *tatlagan-ayaz*, on the other hand, involved living with herds in rural pastures and engaging in the slow practice of interpreting livestock movements. Bilgüün referred to these two educational styles as "like the two chords of the fiddle itself. In order the make the instrument sound right, you have to develop two parallel strings, conservatory education on the right and pastoral education on the left." He used this framing to highlight what he saw as a problem currently facing students. In his words, "The problem we have now is that a lot of young fiddlers have the conservatory side developed and the pastoral side is lacking."

By dictating the appropriate way to engage physically with music, the Party used institutions to implement a modern, socialist rhythm. The rhythm of modernity was a repeatable, rationalized way of engaging with musical transmission that was explicitly disentangled from the unpredictable and flexible rhythms of livestock animals, weather, and fodder growth that form the pastoral polyrhythmia.

The Party even regulated the rhythms of the songs themselves. Composer and music theorist Natsagiin Jantsannorov (2006) wrote that Marshal Choibalsan, the Stalinist leader of Mongolia from 1939 to 1952, ordered musicians to update traditional songs, with a particular focus on time signature and tempo. He even quotes Choibalsan as declaring that "the melodies of our old songs are depressingly long. We must replace these songs with beautiful up-tempo melodies" (2006, 45). The imposition of strict, regular meters on the performance of a variety of traditional genres, including *tatlagan-ayaz* and long-song, along with the imposition of transmission via regular, repeatable schedules based out of urban institutions replicated the imposition of industrial production on the rhythms of pastoral life on a different scale.

Bulls and Brigades

Though I have presented these two styles of learning horse fiddle in opposition to one another, in practice many of the middle-aged and older horse fiddlers I interviewed, like Ganbold and Ganaa, were raised at least partially in pastoral settings. They had the opportunity to learn livestock-centric genres in the pasture while also taking lessons in classical music and jazz at urban institutions. Furthermore, they report that leaving the institution temporarily to learn from livestock was not an uncommon practice during the socialist period.

Having never interacted with bulls before entering the conservatory, Ganbold recalled how he set out to live with a cattle-herding family until he felt that he really knew the animals in order to effectively learn how to play bull-based *tatlagan-ayaz*. He had to learn their colorations and temperaments, their methods of physical expression. During the day, he would work as a ranch hand for the family of a local fiddler, paying close attention to how cattle interact with each other in the pasture. In the afternoons he would sit with his back against the family's round-tent and watch the bull come in from the fields until after sunset. He only returned to his life as a fiddler in the city once he felt he could comfortably play the fiddle with an intimate knowledge of cattle's lives and behaviors.

To explain his experiences of learning the song "Mongol Bükh" ("Mongolian Bull"), Ganbold narrated the moods and movements of the bull he learned from as he performs them through the tune's distinct sections. As he told it, "The song begins with the two strings played together, open. This is the '*om zee*,' the clearing breath." To demonstrate, he played the

B-flat and E-flat strings open together, inhaling on the downstroke and exhaling on the upstroke. He then went on to break down the song into five sections:

A1 is slow, the bull is searching for his flock. He is pawing the earth with his hoof and grunting.

B1 is quick, the bull has found his flock and is trotting over to them.

Back to A1, slow again. The bull has found his mate and is expressing his joy.

B2 picks up the tempo again and doubles the ornamental notes. The bull is driving his mate out into the pasture.

C is a slow, but brief ending to the song that draws out the grunts into low bellows, which ultimately lead to a second *om zee*, which means the song is over.

Through repeated observations and interactions with a herd of cattle, Ganbold developed a set of rhythms which inform his performance. This learning experience required him to flout the expected yearly rhythm of the socialist institution. For Ganbold and other horse fiddlers based out of urban conservatories, temporary leaves of absence to stay in a rural pastoral encampment like this were often sudden and without predetermined end dates. The development of this kind of interspecies empathy does not operate on an institutional timeline, dependent as it is on the social worlds of nonhumans. Just as the time signatures of *tatlagan-ayaz* resist standardization into classical music education, the rhythms of nonhuman animals disrupt the neatly structured rhythms of music education institutions.

One of the major goals of socialist-era music institutionalization was to expand state ideologies even to the most remote areas of the country. Performances on local stages in province centers were originally intended as a way of centralizing musical performance and removing it from the pastoral context. However, to reach remote settlements and support themselves with supplemental income, by the 1980s Ulaanbaatar-based national ensembles had begun breaking up their troupes into smaller *brigats* (brigades) and sending them to perform at *khot ail*, small rural communities formed of pastoral encampments.

Erdene, a former member of one of these ensembles, reported that he learned many *tatlagan-ayaz* on these tours. In my interview with him he pulled down an *igel*, a two-stringed fiddle similar in construction to the horse fiddle, from above the family piano as he described his experience with the *brigats*. He said these home visits brought the institutional form of musical performance to pastoral environs. *Khot ail*, he continued while tuning his instrument, are set up in remote areas to serve the needs of their herds, particularly horses and goats, which need to be pastured carefully because of their particular manners of grazing. As he told me, "horses can pull up grass by the root and goats have sharp hooves that dig into thin soil, so you have to choose where to send them to graze to protect the health of the steppe."

Erdene may well have been referring to Ulaan Ger (Red Houses) or other similar musical institutions set up during the socialist period to centralize and institutionalize rural musical performance. However, he did not use that term, or any other terms, for rural musical institutions of the socialist era such as Ulaan Bulan (Red Corner) or Soyolyn Töv (Cultural Center). He exclusively used the term *khot ail*, emphasizing the domestic, pastoral space rather than the institutional space.

Erdene reported that these trips were his primary way of learning *tatlagan-ayaz*. Having finished tuning the *igel* at this point in the interview, he began to demonstrate one, the very same bull song that Ganbold once set out to learn on his own from a cattle-herding family. After he finished playing, Erdene told me, "I'm a city guy, I didn't know about *tatlagan-ayaz*. So whenever we went out on *brigats*, I would try to learn something new."

While the Party's intention may have been a unidirectional dissemination of officially sanctioned national culture from the center to the periphery, Erdene recalls these performances as opportunities to exchange information with local herders. Furthermore, by re-centering the rural pastoral encampment in musical performance, urban-based performers like him had the opportunity to develop the sensibilities required for *tatlagan-ayaz* by interfacing with livestock that they do not normally engage with. In this case, nonhuman animals participate in an exchange of knowledge, and they also set the meeting conditions of this exchange by having specific pasturing needs that are not easily transposable into the socialist metropole.

Postsocialist Rhythms

After 1990, the rhythms of Mongolian social life changed drastically. As part of the transition away from a single-party socialist state, the Mongolian government implemented a new set of policies designed to re-modernize the country in preparation for entering the global free market economy as a parliamentary democracy (Ginsburg 1995). The adoption of neoliberal policies during this period has led to the dramatic urbanization of the population from rural areas toward the capital city, Ulaanbaatar (Yi and Shi 2016; Cui et al. 2019). The teachers I worked with have to work around another effect of the country's neoliberal policies: a drop in funding for arts education, pushing the teachers to find other lines of support through second careers and personal loans.

As Mongolia moved into the global economy, cashmere became the country's third-largest export (El Benni and Reviron 2009), leading herders to shift away from mixed flocks for meat and dairy production with a full range of five snouts (horses, cattle, camels, goats, and sheep) to an increased focus on goats. The transition to a market economy has resulted in the incursion of Western mining corporations with predatory contracts. This shift in herd composition and widespread formal and informal mining, along with an increasingly arid atmosphere and warm temperatures due to anthropogenic climate change, have led to an increased rate of pasture degradation (Sheehy and Damiran 2012; Mijiddorj et al. 2019). The pasture degradation by mandatory sedentarization and widespread implementation of agriculture further south in the Gobi by the Chinese government in the mid-twentieth century (Humphrey and Sneath 1999) has also started creeping north, threatening pastures on the Mongolian side of the border which had previously been well maintained by nomads. For the traditional musicians I interviewed both in Ulaanbaatar and the rural Gobi, increasing desertification was a major concern.

To herders in Dundgovi, the increasing transformation of semi-arid steppe into desert poses serious concerns for finding renewable forage and water sources for their livestock, particularly for the horses and camels which are pastured closer to the Gobi than sheep, goats, and cattle which can be kept close to the encampment. Beyond the obvious difficulties droughts and desertification pose to maintaining livestock health, these ecological concerns have been making rural-based musical transmission more difficult as well. Fernández-Giménez et al. (2017) warn that the degeneration of these pastures may lead to a "cultural tipping point" where herders leave pastoral lifestyles to the point that pastoral practice cannot be revitalized (65). This is true of musical traditions as well, as rural teachers like Dad'süren and Buyaa struggle to find students to whom to teach horse fiddle and long-song.

Despite the uncertain future of rural pastures and the livestock that populate them, the rise of cultural heritage tourism has increased the demand for horse fiddlers who can evoke a pastoral sound that is markedly different from the modernist, classical style. The element of audible, but palatable, difference from modern conservatory aesthetics is a valuable aspect of heritage music. Writing on traditional musicians in Southwestern China, Rees (1998) found that the musicians she spoke with consciously developed performance styles that appealed to Western tourists' desire to break with modernity. There is both a domestic and a foreign consumer base that wants a similar form of "authenticity" from traditional Mongolian music. Between institutional and pastoral rhythms, there is the potential for what Lefebvre refers to as "arrhythmia," conflict arising from the incompatibility of two or more rhythms (2004). The conundrum, then, is how do horse fiddle teachers and students overcome the increasing arrhythmia between urban and rural life as the need for difference increases and the capacity for the cultivation of that difference decreases?

Horse Fiddle without Horses

For all the changes brought by democratization, many music education and performance institutions established during the socialist period have maintained their role as the primary centers of traditional music professionalization. The Music and Dance College lives on today as the National Conservatory, and most people still refer to it by its old name. Though the institutions of horse fiddle education from the socialist era remain, the conditions of postsocialism have made it more difficult for students to pursue parallel music training in pastoral contexts. Increasing urbanization and environmental degradation have made nomadic pastures less accessible to the new generation of fiddle students. This social distance from livestock is a significant area of consternation for those middle-aged and older fiddle teachers who feel that their urban-based students have a disadvantage when trying to learn livestock-centric genres.

In response to this concern, a group of music teachers from the State University of Arts and Culture, the National Conservatory, and the National Horse fiddle Ensemble have teamed up to start master classes for horse fiddle students to develop their techniques for *tatlagan-ayaz* and other traditional genres. These fiddle teachers are experimenting with ways to bring pastoral elements into urban, institutional music education. For the first master class, the director wanted to bring in a rural herder-musician like Dad'süren to teach a group of Music and Dance College students. However, the fiddlers they reached out to refused to come, citing air pollution and expense as reasons to stay away from the city. As Dad'süren once told me, "Ulaanbaatar is a foreign country to me."

A performer from the State Horse Fiddle Ensemble stepped in to teach the first master class. The master class packed a performance room in the new wing of the Music and Dance College. An after-hours and noncredit course, its high attendance demonstrated a genuine desire on the part of fiddle students for more education in pastoral approaches to playing the instrument. Throughout the master class, the teacher urged students to seek out and learn from nature in their current surroundings. He warned them that what they learned in school could prepare them to be good classical musicians, but it would not prepare them to be great fiddlers. Though his students attentively followed along, he became progressively more frustrated throughout the course. When I asked him about the class later, he told me that he felt like he was grasping at straws trying to find ways to teach students how to play a horse's gait without a horse.

After the class, I found the director again to ask him if he considered this first master class successful. In frustration, he threw up his hand and sharply retorted, "I wouldn't say it was much of a master class at all, would you?" He brushed past me without waiting for a response but turned back to say, "If we can't bring the country to the city, we'll just have to send the students to the country!" He considered the master class a failure and that any course that depended on the institutional rhythm, the seminar in an urban conservatory, was doomed to fail in the same way.

Though expressed in frustration, the idea of sending urban-based students to engage with rural, pastoral lifeways is not without precedent. A voice professor at the Arts and Culture University has found success teaching her long-song students landscape-based singing by taking them on field trips to various rural landscapes to learn to sing with the land. This approach has caught on, first adopted by a polyphonic throat singing professor in the same department and then later as part of a "rural economy life skills" (*khödöö aj akhui*) curriculum practiced at a handful of private horse fiddle schools.

There is a parallel between this plan and the earlier practice of *brigats*, shipping urban-based fiddle performers to rural pastoral encampments. This plan is partially a reversal in that fiddlers would be sent to learn from herders and herds rather than perform for them. However, the conditions of postsocialism make previously standard plans less feasible. The problems of the neoliberalization of the country make these kinds of trips nonviable. No funding is available to send a group of students with their instruments to a rural pasture.

By the time I left Mongolia in 2018, no educational field trips for the horse fiddle students had been organized. The professors in charge cited incredible difficulty finding funding, transportation, and housing for their students and their fiddles. The transition from a state-planned economy to free market capitalism has left a gulf in financial and organizational support for public projects, including arts education. Teachers and students are left with a uniquely postsocialist problem of making a socialist structure operate within a capitalist system.

These master classes indicate a sincere desire among teachers and students to incorporate techniques and aesthetics for performing *tatlagan-ayaz*, otherwise unavailable within classical music institutions. However, the teachers expressed frustration that their master classes could not succeed without access to horses, camels, and bulls. This frustration points to an inability of the urban institution in its current form to fully absorb or replace the roles of nonhuman animals in music education. Nonhumans perform their rhythms through their bodies, simultaneously reacting to and constructing space as they move through it. These bodily rhythms are vital aspects of *tatlagan-ayaz* that the horse fiddle teachers maintained must be learned in the pastoral context.

Back to the Pasture

Back at the National Conservatory, Ganbold told me that one of his students, whom he had not heard from for six weeks, had returned to his private lessons. This student, Mönkherdene, a self-described lifelong urbanite, grew up on the outskirts of Ulaanbaatar. Though he stepped away from the conservatory for over a month without warning in his last year before graduating, Ganbold did not seem upset with him. To the contrary, he was beaming.

Mönkherdene left the city to work as a seasonal assistant herder. Toward the end of summer, herders in the grasslands in the northeastern provinces look for extra hands to gather grass to dry and store in Ulaanbaatar as insurance against increasingly common and severe winter disasters that cause large-scale livestock starvation. Mönkherdene said that he took this job to be close to horses, to help him learn a *tatlagan-ayaz* called "Guilgee" ("Full Gallop"). He told us that he taught himself this song by paying close attention to the horses as they galloped during the day and by listening to his recording of Ganbold on his phone at night. "He went out on his own to do this," Ganbold exclaimed excitedly. "Now, that is the only way to learn this music!"

Taking this advice, I decided to follow in Mönkherdene's footsteps and take a trip to a rural pasture to learn a *tatlagan-ayaz* myself. I met with Ganbold at the Music and Dance College at the end of the winter to ask how I should prepare for my upcoming trip to the rural Gobi for the spring. He led me down a winding path around the newly constructed wing of the conservatory, to the back of the compound where the old socialist-era school still stands, hidden from the street. Ganbold ushered me to a two-floor wooden cabin off to the side of the complex, the only building on site not built in the Soviet, yellowish concrete slab style.

Standing in the cold, Ganbold flipped through a keyring and told me, "This is the old singing classroom." Inside, the walls were lined with framed photos of vocal teachers at pianos from the formative early years of the college. He showed me to an old classroom that has recently been repurposed by students who are starting a folk-rock band. A young music instructor sat at a table in the corner, quietly carving a large pile of overtone flutes called *tsuur* out of PVC pipe.

I could not help but notice that this space has its own rhythm. It was a refuge for people to develop their music and career prospects in parallel with the conservatory. Using this space to practice, hold private lessons, or work with foreign researchers after school hours, musicians engaged in a near rhythm of conservatory work. They came to the same complex, played music, and built and repaired instruments in otherwise abandoned buildings, at odd hours, with space heaters to combat the lack of insulation and heating. These buildings were kept locked, so an instructor or a guard would have to approve these activities for them to continue.

Setting up two chairs next to the space heater, Ganbold started to advise me on what to ask for and pay attention to, both for my research and my development as a horse fiddler. He told me that the most important thing would be to watch the camels, to see how they run, and to listen to how they bellow into the night when they come to nuzzle their calves. This trip would be a chance for me to learn how to play a *tatlagan-ayaz* that evokes the characteristics of a camel, "Builgan Sharyn Yavdal" ("Gait of the Bridled Yellow [Camel]"). Though I had previously attempted to learn the song, I had never really grasped it. Ganbold insisted that being able to call upon a real, embodied knowledge of how camels move and bellow was necessary for me to play it correctly.

A month or so later, I stood out in front of my hosts' felt tent in the northern Gobi. It was our first night at the spring pasture, having set up the encampment the day before and finished up with the fence-mending this morning. Throughout the day, as we carried out herding chores, such as watering the sheep, I tried to pay attention to the way the camels trotted, shambled, and heaved their way through the dusty steppe. The male camels were out to pasture in "the Gobi," which is the term my hosts used for rural grazing spots deep enough into the semi-desert as to be too hostile to encamp. This group of camels was allowed to wander, with herders only checking on them periodically. Herders keep recent mother camels and their calves close to the encampment to account for the new mothers' tendency to reject their young and leave them to fend for themselves (figure 1). The camels jogged into the steppe each morning to search for food. The calves were left behind.

Each day, I watched the camels as they charged into the steppe, taking long strides with their heads tossed back. Approaching, the camels' thick, reddish-brown neck beards, left to grow throughout the winter, swayed side to side in response to their heavy gait. Departing, they kicked up great clouds of dust that followed them deep into the pasture.

After the mother camels left, one of my hosts, Byambaa, and I started cleaning up the fenced enclosures to prepare them for the sheep and goats, who would soon be birthing. The camel calves sat together nearby, tied to stakes in the ground to keep them from wandering off before they are

FIGURE 1 Mother camels and calves kept close to the encampment. Dundgovi, Mongolia. Photograph by K. G. Hutchins.

strong enough to survive on their own in the steppe. The countryside is often quiet but rarely silent, as joking, gossiping, whistling, singing, spitting, and laughing create a persistent soundscape. But when Byambaa shouted from among the calves, everyone fell silent.

Even the camels stopped bellowing and turned to stare expectantly at Byambaa as he pushed through them to a calf who had fallen to the ground and stopped moving. Byambaa approached and disentangled the calf from the hitching line around the animal's neck, thinking him dead. Just as he got the still limp calf free, it sprung up and started prancing away, bouncing on the tips of its toes and lifting its knees high, barking out a kind of triumphant laughter.

This calf was dramatic. He would wail and kick his feet when he felt restless, tied to his hitching line. Several times throughout the spring, he wrapped himself up in the tether and fell to the ground, playing dead and teasing his herders.

Around dusk each night, a chill wind carried a mixture of Gobi scents to the encampment—goat and sheep musk, burning dung and fur from the trash pile, and the robust and prickly taste-aroma of sage. It was quite cold at night that early in spring, even in the Gobi. The mother camels nuzzled up with their calves and formed a wall of body and fur against the night winds. Each evening, once they had settled in, the mother camels arched their long, fuzzy necks back and bellowed—long, warbling, deep and booming cries that carried over the steppe. The camels' song sounded, to my ears, mournful and nostalgic, yet protective all the same. Through interacting with the camels throughout the spring, I learned that to perform a convincing bellow on the horse fiddle's strings, the fiddler must call to mind the loving, often fraught relationship between the mother and calf.

After these observations, I made several adjustments to my playing style. Small changes had significant effects on the sound of the piece. For example, I adapted the dust-drawing, strike-pull-coil motion I saw camels take with their strides into my left-hand technique, adding a bouncy, thrumming element to the performance. More significantly, I attempted to re-create Ganbold's method of breaking down the *tatlagan-ayaz* into sections derived from the animals' different rhythms. Here is a representation of how the observations I made of these camels informed my performance of "Builgan Sharyn Yavdal":

I begin with the *om zee*, breathing in on the downstroke and out on the upstroke. Rather than B-flat and E-flat, this song opens with B-flat and F.

Section A starts at a medium pace, very deliberate. The camel is starting
   off into the steppe, beard swaying side to side.
B is strong and loud, evoking a joyous camel's high-stepping, playful
   trot.
C pushes the song to a higher register and alternates between the left
   and right strings as the camel's humps sway side to side when it picks
   up speed.
D is quiet as the camel runs off into the steppe. Picking up on
   Dad'süren's performance from the *nair*, I take this section as a time
   to break away from standard time, allowing the camel in the song to
   trail off.
E ends with the bellow before returning to a second *om zee* to finish the
   song.

When I returned to Ulaanbaatar, I played "Builgan Sharyn Yavdal" for Ganbold again, using what I had learned from watching the camels.

Ganbold was satisfied that I had finally turned a corner, going from simply "playing notes" to "actually performing." "Builgan Sharyn Yavdal" would become my go-to song to play for friends and host family members for the rest of my time in Mongolia. Friends would call on me to play this song for Lunar New Year's celebrations to fulfill the "*javar ürgeekh,*" the ritual "lifting of the chill" that I mentioned in the previous chapter. Learning from the camels in Dundgovi turned my performance of the fiddle from a curiosity into a potential for carrying out this culturally and spiritually significant ritual.

Conclusion

My chilly nights rehearsing with the Horse Fiddle Symphony left me with the question of how nonhuman animals can act as teachers of music in a conservatory system that is based on a separation of "nature" from "culture." Answering this question took me out of the conservatory, out of the capital, and into the pasture in Dundgovi province. There I found that the rhythms that horses, camels, and cattle perform through their bodily engagements with the steppe are necessary elements of *tatlagan-ayaz* education that disrupt the urban-based rhythms of conservatory education without destabilizing them.

During the twentieth century, the state enshrined the horse fiddle as national music for the nascent People's Republic of Mongolia and moved the locus of its instruction to Soviet-style institutions that followed sedentary, European rhythms. This project was designed to distance the music and the people who played it from nomadism. However, fiddlers found ways to bring nomadic elements into the conservatory, using institutional time and resources to pursue animal-based learning and composition.

Into the twenty-first century, the shift to neoliberalism has left these Soviet-style institutions still standing, but underfunded. The concept of "national music" was supplanted by "cultural heritage," but the same institutions oversee the instruction of heritage instruments like the horse fiddle. The rhythms of neoliberal life are more totalizing, more isolating, and give performers fewer opportunities to find nomadic pastures to spend time developing their musical acumen within. Despite the increased difficulty and reduced state support, fiddlers still strive to bring the sounds of horses into the conservatory.

These conundrums that horse fiddle instructors deal with in the classroom are reflections of overarching issues. Life for Indigenous people in postsocialist Asia means navigating a mess of disjointed societal rhythms that have been imposed, directly and indirectly, by colonial forces continually reproducing their disparate versions of modernity through political and economic pressure on smaller, less powerful communities. If there is any eurythmia to be found at the disjuncture between the leftover rhythms of Soviet institutional life and the freneticism of neoliberalism's profit-driven rhythms, it will be in finding ways to bring counter-hegemonic ways of knowing in through the cracks left by the two modernities' incongruities. For horse fiddlers, the formal incorporation of the fiddle into modernist projects, first as national music and then again as heritage, allows them to work nomadic rhythms into the institution.

Time in rural pastures is necessary for developing skill on the horse fiddle, at least according to the fiddlers like Ganbold and Ganaa. The following chapter goes deeper into how people relate to nonhuman animals through music in those nomadic contexts. While staying in Dundgovi to try to develop my camel-based fiddling for "Builgan Sharyn Yavdal," I found that some herders use music as a form of caretaking for their livestock. While in this chapter I examined situations in which nonhuman animals served as inspiration for musical performance, in the following chapter I take cases of herders' using song as a herding tool as an opportunity to examine what it means for animals to be critical consumers of music.

CHAPTER 3

LIKE A LULLABY

Toward the end of winter, I mentioned to my friend Pürev my desire to go back down to Dundgovi to learn *tatlagan-ayaz*. He told me that it was good timing, because he was going down at the beginning of spring and taking a couple of guys from his job to help out his cousins set up the spring encampment for his family's livestock. He said if I wanted to, I could go down with him and stay on for the spring livestock birthing season and then catch a mail bus back to the city at the end of April.

A few days later I met up with another buddy, Batka, and told him about my plan over a couple of beers. Like Pürev, Batka spends most of the year in the city but travels to help his relatives take care of pastoral duties several times a year. I had just gone on one such trip with him a few weeks earlier to bring hay from a storage unit in Ulaanbaatar to help his cousins' cattle survive a nasty winter storm in rural Töv province. Batka told me, "Going in the spring, eh? You are about to learn something the hard way." He then wrote something on a notepad and smacked it down on the table in front of me. It read, "LAW OF LIFE."

Spring in the Mongolian Gobi is a short and intense season of strong winds, dust storms, and wild temperature changes. It is also the birthing season for livestock, a critical period for herders fraught with challenges for animals and humans alike. Due to the difficult weather of this period and the strain on livestock weakened from the winter, it is common for mothers to die and for newborn animals to be orphaned. "To see things die, this is the law of life," Batka told me.

The birthing season brings other problems as well. Some of the new mothers who survive reject their own newborns and refuse to nurse them. When new lambs are orphaned or abandoned, the herders I worked with in Dundgovi province sing the animals species-specific, semi-improvisational songs to help bond the baby animal to a mother and encourage her to nurse. When used with sheep and lambs, this practice is called *toiglokh* after the vocable *toig*, which forms the lyrical basis of the genre.

The version of this practice reserved for reuniting camel calves with their mothers, called *khööslökh*, has received increasing international attention lately. Byambasüren Davaa's docudrama *The Story of the Weeping Camel* brought the practice to the world stage in 2003. In 2015 it was inscribed on UNESCO's List of Intangible Cultural Heritage in Need of Urgent Safeguarding for Mongolia under the name "Coaxing Ritual for Camels."

Surviving the ecological precarity of neoliberalism depends on multispecies entanglement, the mutual interdependence of humans, animals, and others across species boundaries (Tsing 2015). Byambaa relies on his sheep to provide his livelihood with their milk, meat, and wool. The sheep depend on him in return for care and protection. The sheep even depend on the goats. As Batka told me, "You have to herd sheep and goats together. Without the goats to keep them moving, the sheep will lie down and forget to eat."

This style of singing is a herding tool, a method of cross-species communication, and a form of musical cultural heritage. Through our collaborative, cross-species engagements, human beings deeply, inextricably entangle with other animals (Haraway 2008). Singing is one of those collaborative engagements through which multispecies entangling is possible.

The sounds of the songs that herders sing are recognizable as music for human enjoyment in one context and as an animal herding tool in another. However, the way performers sing for sheep has an effect on the way they sing for people, and vice versa. Musical herding practices, in which human and animal sociality are brought together, open a space for us to consider how humans and nonhuman animals coproduce one another through artistic performance. Taking music-making as a form of multispecies engagement, I consider instances of this practice of singing to livestock to promote nursing to be contexts for interspecies bonding and social development that influence human-animal, human-human, and animal-animal relationships that extend beyond the context of the musical performance itself.

Animals and Music

Nonhuman animals play multiple key roles in the composition and performance of music in pastoral contexts. Herders' use of song and instrumental music for calling to livestock and warding off predators assign a limited kind of audience role to herds, as they react to human calls and respond to voices they recognize (Campbell 1951; Ivarsdotter 2004; Johnson 1984). In nomadic Inner Asia, animals take part in the composition of music, as people use mimetic performances of animal-derived song to achieve both mundane and spiritual ends (Levin and Süzükei 2006; Pegg 2001).

Traditional ecological knowledge, including the use of song as a herding tool, is an integral part of ecosystem management in precarious ecologies (Anderson 1996; Berkes, Colding, and Folke 2000; Turner, Ignace, and Ignace 2000; Lepofsky 2009). Recent considerations of the interaction between artistic production and ecological management (Curtis 2006; Tucker 2016), along with theoretical movements toward the integration of ontology into biology (Daly et al. 2016), push researchers to examine the full webs of relationality at play in multispecies musical engagements. The multispecies approach requires us to open up anthropocentric concepts to the possibility of nonhuman participants. If penguins and flying foxes are capable of creating narratives and imbuing places with storied meaning (Van Dooren and Bird Rose 2012), we can also take the possibility of sheep being critical consumers of music seriously.

The daily practices of animal domestication have effects on the inner worlds of the humans and nonhumans involved, transforming the identities of both (Despret 2004, 130–31). Taking care of domestic animals is a series of intimate acts through which humans create interspecies kinship relationships (Haraway 2003; Govindrajan 2018). Singing to sheep as a way of bringing together an orphaned lamb with a new mother is a form of care, marked with the familial intimacy of a lullaby.

In this chapter, I take sheep as having a kind of agency as critical consumers of music. Scholars have written about music as a site for multispecies communication and collaboration between humans and nonhuman animals, with a particular focus on how humans interpret and respond to the sounds of other animals (Nollman 1999; Rothenberg 2008; Simonett 2015). In Dundgovi, nonhuman animals' consumption and responses to human-composed music are also important.

For the herders I worked with in Dundgovi, observing and understanding how sheep respond to their singing is an important part of maintaining the health of their herds. Reflecting on these experiences, herders engage in discourses that theorize the animals' capacity as an engaged audience for human-produced music. Through acts of musical performance, heritage bearers bring together the social worlds of humans and sheep in this rural Dundgovi pasture. The affective power of song draws humans into the intimate world of mother-child relationships among domestic sheep.

Spring and Fall in the Gobi

Dundgovi is a province on the northern side of the Gobi in central Mongolia. As you travel south, its arid, grassy steppe gives way to sage and saxaul semi-desert (figure 2). Spring in the Gobi, though short, is a critical season for herders and their herds. A roughly forty-five-day stretch from mid-March until the end of April marks the birthing season for livestock. Dust storms and nightly freezes, along with the weakened state of the animals after a long and difficult winter, complicate this already dangerous period.

Livestock finish birthing by the end of spring and fatten throughout the summer, so that by autumn herds are at their most calm and stable. At the end of summer and the beginning of fall, horses provide milk that can be fermented into a refreshing, mildly alcoholic beverage called *airag*. Fall weather is mild and temperate. A counterbalance to the stresses of spring, fall is a time for celebrations that involve other kinds of singing and music-making that intersect with the practice of livestock-singing in ways that bring the emotional worlds of nonhumans into human-centric performance contexts.

FIGURE 2 Dundgovi in the spring with nursing sheep and lambs. Photograph by K. G. Hutchins.

Though there are many species of livestock raised in Dundgovi, most of the herds in the province are made up of the *tavan khoshuu mal*, the "five snouts" of traditionally herded domesticated ungulates: sheep (*Ovis aries*), goats (*Capra aegagrus hircus*), cattle (*Bos taurus*), horses (*Equus ferus caballus*), and Bactrian camels (*Camelus bactrianus*). For each of the five snouts, there is a specific nursing song, with its own words and melodies. Though the melodies and lyrics herders use to sing to livestock change from pasture to pasture throughout Mongolia (Pegg 2001; Fijn 2011; Biraa 2017), in the county where I did my research, *toig* was the word for sheep, *tsii* or *tsee* was for goats, *öög* was for cattle, *khöös* was for camels, and *gürii* was for horses. These are vocables, words with no lexical meaning in conversation but special use in song. Their function is solely to sooth the animals. In this chapter, I focus on the term *toig* and the practice of *toiglokh*, the general term for the practice of singing for sheep. This is the example I have the most experience with and has been the one most commonly used by herders with whom I worked.

I will start by detailing the use of springtime livestock-singing with nursing sheep by two brothers in their late thirties to early forties, whom

I will call Byambaa and Mandaa. Then, I turn to three herders and singers in their seventies and eighties, experts in a variety of traditional herding practices and musical genres, especially *urtyn duu*, whom I will refer to as Buyaa, Naraa, and Dad'süren. I draw upon experiences and interviews with them at different points in the year, exploring how they relate the human-livestock interactions of springtime with their human-centric traditional musical performances in the fall. We return to the fall *nair* at Gombo's encampment, where Buyaa and Dad'süren first introduced me to the idea that the horses were also part of the music.

During the spring, I participated in pastoral labor, acting as an additional (if ineffective) pair of hands during a period when many urban-based relatives join herders for the difficult work of moving the encampment from winter to spring pasture and helping with new mothers and lambs. Like any other fiddle student taking a break from the conservatory to learn a *tatlagan-ayaz*, I used this ranch hand work as an opportunity to observe the rhythms of horses and camels. While working with the herders, I noticed that musical engagement formed a part of everyday pastoral practices.

During the following fall, I came back to this county to participate in *nair*, day-long traditional celebrations defined by singing and drinking fermented mare's milk. These *nair* were sites of the performance and intergenerational transmission of long-song, a genre of music that has a close relationship with livestock-singing in the province.

As the efficacy of music herding techniques relies not just on herders' abilities to affect their wills upon sheep, but also on their abilities to foster enduring care relationships between new mother sheep and lambs, I took a multispecies approach with my participant-observation. I paid special attention to times and places where human and nonhuman socialities overlap, such as the sheep corral at dusk when the herds are brought home from the pasture and orphaned lambs are brought together with new mothers. Two of my hosts, Mandaa and Buyaa, gave me instruction on how they read interactions between livestock and engage empathetically with them.

Byambaa and Mandaa were both raised in this county in rural Dundgovi province and learned herding from a young age. They moved out of the province to work in the city for several years before returning to the Gobi to take care of the family flocks of livestock after their eldest sister and her husband retired from herding. The family raises an expansive herd of the full range of the five snouts. Responsibility for the herds is spread among various siblings and cousins throughout the county, though Byambaa and Mandaa take care of a large share, with a few hundred sheep and goats staying in the fenced enclosures next to the small, felt round-tent that they share and the cattle pasturing nearby.

In the middle of March, I traveled down to Dundgovi with Pürev as planned to help Byambaa and Mandaa move their encampment. We disassembled their felt home on their winter pasture, where they had been staying for several months, placed it on the back of a pick-up truck, and reconfigured it on their spring pasture nearby. Within a few days of us moving the pasture and setting up a fenced enclosure for the sheep and goats to stay in at night, the expectant mothers began to give birth to lambs and kids.

In the first week, one of the mother sheep died giving birth. Her lamb survived. Byambaa brought the orphaned lamb beyond a second set of fences within the sheep enclosure, where a few nursing sheep and lambs had already been separated from the rest of the flock (figure 3). He left the lamb to stay with the other newborns and new mothers for the rest of the day. Around sunset, after he and Mandaa brought the sheep back from the pasture to their encampment, he returned to the mothers' circle. Dusk is a vital time for newborns to enter the care of their mothers; if they are not fed and accepted, they will have a hard time surviving the night, as temperatures fall below freezing and the wind picks up. He fed a rope through the back of the enclosure so that we could tie one of the nursing mothers to the back fence. He selected a sheep who had recently given birth but seemed hearty and healthy enough to support another lamb and squatted next to her, looping his left arm around the mother's neck and holding the lamb close with his right. After a few moments of quiet reassurances, he began singing "*toi-toi-toi-guu ee-khe-khe-khee ee-ye-ee.*"

Byambaa continued to sing like this, with variations on the melody and ornamentation until long after the sun set. He paused only to shout for me to bring him a flashlight so that he could continue to make sure that the lamb stayed in the right position to nurse in the dark. Later that night he told me that he would continue to repeat this process of bringing the orphan together with the mother and singing to them at sunset until the new mother accepted the baby as her own and cared for it without

FIGURE 3 Sheep enclosure with fenced area for new mothers and lambs. Photograph by K. G. Hutchins.

his direction. On the first night, he sang to this pair for over half an hour before the sheep nursed and thereby brought the *toiglokh* to a successful conclusion. However, on the second night, it took only a couple of minutes for the sheep to take to the lamb. After two evenings of *toiglokh*, Byambaa decided that the sheep and lamb were ready to be reintegrated into the herd as a mother-child pair.

Once the sheep and lamb were reintegrated into the herd, they behaved like any other mother-child pair. The lamb followed the mother and called to her when in distress, and the mother responded with care and concern. The new mother interacted with this adopted lamb just as she did with the lamb to which she had given birth, and her relationship with that lamb seemed to be largely unchanged. Though Byambaa engineered this relationship by separating the mother sheep and lamb from the rest of the herd and singing to them over the course of a couple of evenings, the mother sheep and adopted lamb developed a caring, trusting relationship that extended outside of the space and time of the *toiglokh* performance itself. Through acts of care, humans build kin-like relations with nonhuman animals (Govindrajan 2018). Byambaa uses traditional song as a form of care to create kinship not just between himself and the sheep, but to build kin relations between the sheep and lamb as well.

Byambaa continued taking sheep aside and singing to them each evening for the next couple of weeks, using *toiglokh* to adopt a handful of lambs to new mothers throughout the rest of the birthing season. He explained that the singing itself is what makes the sheep nurse and that the singing calms the sheep and lamb. In conjunction with the pair's confinement to the secondary enclosure and isolation from the herd, the singing made the animals comfortable with each other's presence.

Byambaa was not alone in voicing this perspective. The idea that singing calms sheep and causes them to nurse came through in each of my interviews with herders from around the county for the rest of the spring. Singing in this area was such a useful tool for promoting nursing that many of the people I worked with report that they sing while milking as well.

Later that spring, I asked Buyaa if there are other methods for handling child rejection among livestock, but he told me, "No, just *toiglokh*." Though in other pastures throughout Mongolia, and the Central Asian steppe more broadly, pastoralists may engage in a wide variety of sheep adoption practices, in this county in rural Dundgovi province, my interlocutors stressed that singing is their sole method. If there are other techniques, Byambaa and Mandaa did not need them that year; of the seven lambs adopted to new mothers through the use of *toiglokh*, only one adopted mother rejected her new lamb after being reintegrated into the herd.

In this case, *toiglokh* is a pastoral tool and an affective practice. Wealth and stability for pastoralists are tied up in the material reproduction of the animals themselves (Ingold 1988). An orphaned or abandoned lamb represents a liability to Byambaa and his family's economic well-being. As a tool of domestication, *toiglokh* addresses an economic problem for Byambaa, as an orphaned or rejected lamb is a threat to the reproduction of the herd.

However, the effect Byambaa was attempting to instill is an affective one. Affect is the unconscious response to an external stimulus (Spinoza and Curley 1985). Here we do not need to worry about the emotional inner worlds of nonhuman animals or even their ability to understand the music that they are hearing because affect is a bodily response. Affect is not emotion, as it is presocial (Shouse 2005), nor does it depend on cognition, as it is a precognitive response (Massumi 1995). Byambaa has empirical evidence that the sheep respond affectively to his singing when the mother accepts the lamb and the lamb begins to nurse. He reads the physiological states of anxiety and calm, using song to bring the sheep from the first state to the second. The body's responses to outside stimuli include responses to pasts, to traces of events and understandings that have happened repeatedly in the past (Massumi 1995). Through the repetition of this ritual action, Byambaa enfolds the context of the ritual into the affective responses of the sheep.

Addressing problems across species boundaries requires attention to affect. Herders depend on reading the animals' physical responses to stimuli and being able to provide contexts that will produce desired autonomous physiological responses. So, the solution consists of affective mechanisms—repeated physical engagements of sound and touch in a consistent, separated location within the corral. Byambaa used song to impart a relaxed sensation on the mother sheep and lamb in the hopes that it will instill in the two animals a physical response similar to comfort when they are in the presence of one another. Once he reintegrated the animals back into the herd, he depended on the sheep and lamb to build upon those feelings. It is the music, and the herder and sheep's shared ability to engage affectively with it, that allows for this domestication practice to take place. The emotional impact on the sheep and lamb, and the relationship that they maintain after reintegration, are what make *toiglokh* a functional tool for maintaining the herd.

The 2016 report on Mongolian Intangible Cultural Heritage to UNESCO describes livestock-singing in other parts of Mongolia as a "monotone chant" (Huh 2016). In Dundgovi, some herders did indeed perform the song this way. For example, Byambaa's brother Mandaa had a very chant-like style, as he repeated "*toig-uu*" with the same high-low pitch movement. However, Byambaa's form of *toiglokh* traced a dynamic melody that rose briefly before plunging low, finally driving up in pitch and volume in a stirring crescendo, punctuated by a pulsing vibrato ornamentation. His *toiglokh* was stylistically similar to another form of Mongolian traditional music, long-song.

Elements of Long-Song in Pastoral Practice

Long-song is a genre of vocal performance characterized by dense poetic texts sung through long, highly ornamented and semi-improvisational melodies. Unlike *toiglokh* and other livestock coaxing music, long-song is a performative art style intended for human audiences, with deep philosophical texts and soaring melodies. Listening to Byambaa as he performed the *toiglokh* for the orphaned lamb and her new mother, I could hear discrete ornamentations and melodic runs from long-song. When I asked him about it later that night, he told me at first that he does not consider himself a singer, though he admitted to knowing a song or two. When I compared his singing to the chant-like versions of *toiglokh* that I have heard of previously, he offered that Dundgovi herders like him like to sing with a bit of long-song flair.

Byambaa told me that such herders adapt long-song to the space of the sheep enclosure and their nonhuman audience. He himself played with the form of long-song by moving fluidly between chanting and long ornamental runs. He lifted melodies from particular songs and replaced the lyrics with the repeated "*toig toig-uu*," a sound meant specifically to calm sheep. Shifting between recognizable melodies, chanting, and long stretches of ornamental improvisation, Byambaa wove elements from long-song throughout his *toiglokh*.

Byambaa and Mandaa's herds finished birthing relatively early in the season, long before the end of April. With no fences left to patch and no lambs left to birth, Byambaa sent me to stay at Buyaa and Naraa's encampment to work with them and with Dad'süren, who lives in the nearby administrative center of the county. On the way to Buyaa and Naraa's place, Byambaa told me to bring up my questions about long-song and *toiglokh* with these elders. The three of them are well known in the county as excellent singers of *toiglokh*, whose livestock-singing is both effective at calming the animals and aesthetically beautiful. In addition to being expert herders, all three are virtuoso *urtyn duu* singers and teachers.

Long-song, like *toiglokh* and other forms of livestock-singing, is widespread throughout the Mongolian-speaking world and takes a variety of forms (Pegg 2001; Yoon 2013). As such, I do not aim to make a universal claim about its practice or origins. Rather, I am interested in how the particular relationship between *toiglokh* and long-song in Dundgovi invites us to think of nonhuman animals as potential audiences of human music. Dad'süren, a retired herder and the primary traditional music teacher for the county, explained that the relationship between *toiglokh* and long-song in this province is not accidental.

Dad'süren described long-song as a herder's art form, best learned from horseback. A singer must take a special consideration for nonhuman audiences, such as horses and sheep, and for nonhuman sources of inspiration, especially landscape features. In his mid-eighties now, he settled in town and retired from herding, but he still teaches long-song to his apprentices in pastoral contexts. He said that he teaches from the pasture because long-song and *toiglokh* have similar kinds of power. Just as *toiglokh* has the power to move the emotions of the sheep, long-song has the power to move the emotions of people. Sheep and people, he reminded me, are not so different.

Gesturing out the window of his house in the administrative center, Dad'süren directed my attention to the spreading steppe. I looked out the window to see the dusty orange plane of the Gobi, dotted by dark green patches of sage. From this vantage point behind the window in this village, the vastness of the steppe was deceptive, the horizon hemmed in by a wall of mountains. The steppe is so quiet that every noise is amplified, echoing and distorted over the small bumps in the landscape. Every unique sound of wind running over different rocks, every bleat and bellow from distant livestock, every barking dog comes through clearly but distant.

As I took in the view, dust kicking up in a red haze around tiny white flecks of far-off sheep, Dad'süren started again. He told me, "Look at our land, see how it is? It is vast, calm. So our hearts should be: vast, calm. We sing the vastness of the steppe through our song." The extended, meandering melodies, the sharp rises from low, sustained notes to an ethereal falsetto, and striking vocal modulation as ornamentation reflect the landscape features of the steppe and the desert, bringing with them the moral and emotional character of the landscape. Musically, performers use these techniques to instill a sense of steppe-like calm in their audience, whether they are addressing a human audience with long-song or a nonhuman audience with *toiglokh*.

Here, it is important to be clear about the roles different nonhumans played in Dad'süren's explanation. The landscape has a moral and aesthetic character that singers can read and sound through their performance. Sonic constructions and reconstructions of landscapes are well documented as a spiritual practice in Inner Asia (Levin and Süzükei 2006).

Feld (1996) argues that music is a multisensory faculty through which people create place. In doing so, the senses involved in this musical

production become tied to that place in turn. Nonhuman animals participate in this sensing of place as well. Livestock, in this case, participate in
the act of sensing the rural Gobi landscape by acting as critical audiences
for the musical performances of their herders.

Dad'süren attributed much of his skill as a long-song singer to his experiences singing to livestock, saying, "For many years, my only listeners
were the sheep in the field." While Dad'süren drew upon the landscape as
a source of inspiration, he valued sheep as a critical audience for the music. As a teacher, Dad'süren directed students to interpret the landscape
of the Gobi as they sing, but he paid particular attention to how the sheep
and horses respond to the students' performances. Reading the calmness
or agitation of the livestock based on their behavior, he considered their
feedback as an important indicator of the students' merit as singers.

Buyaa and Naraa, a married couple of herders and singers who encamp
near Dad'süren's town, also perform long-song and *toiglokh* in interconnected ways. Like Byambaa and Mandaa, they were raised as herders but
took a long hiatus from pastoralism. Buyaa spent his younger years as a
driver, while Naraa worked as an accountant. Now in their mid-seventies,
they have both retired to the countryside to take up herding again with a
small flock of about one hundred sheep and goats. They are also musicians
and music teachers, performing for local celebrations and passing on *urtyn
duu* and a variety of other traditional praise songs to apprentices throughout the province and beyond, particularly at celebrations during autumn.

Buyaa and Naraa purposefully blend long-song and *toiglokh*. In interviews, they both told me that they choose songs that they sing in the fall
for human audiences and adapt them to sing as *toiglokh* for sheep during
the spring. Buyaa said he is partial to singing "Kheer Khaltar" ("Speckled
Bay Horse") to his herds, replacing the song's verses of poetic text with a
cycle of vocables that he repeats for as long as takes to get the sheep to
nurse. He used the song as the melodic basis for his livestock coaxing and
ornaments his performance with *tsokhilgo*, a modulated vocal pulsation
associated with long-song.

Buyaa explained that he usually chooses a song that moves him to
sing to his livestock. He told me that he sings it because it will sooth the
sheep to hear just as it soothes him to sing. He interprets the responses
of the sheep, noting what calms or agitates them. Singing to sheep is his
primary way of practicing this technically difficult singing style, so that the

aesthetics of what appeals to sheep become a part of his performances for human audiences in the fall.

Buyaa told me that many herders, especially old-timers, have a favorite long-song song they use for helping their sheep nurse. Each herder picks a different song that moves them. While Buyaa himself claimed "Kheer Khaltar" as his favorite tune to sing, he wistfully recalled how, when Dad'süren still herded, he would sing the most beautiful *toiglokh* version of the song "Jargaltain Delger" ("Expanding Joy") for his sheep.

At the *Nair*

As spring passed, Buyaa and Naraa's herds finished birthing as well. The livestock that survived this critical period continued to fatten during the summer. Though there were no more orphaned or rejected lambs to tend to, Byambaa and Mandaa continued to sing to livestock while milking. Just before the beginning of fall and the onset of the festival season, Byambaa's family collected milk from horses to ferment into *airag*. To encourage them to produce milk, Byambaa sang to the mares just as he sang to the sheep and lambs, replacing the sheep-calming sound "*toig*" with a sound meant to calm horses, "*gürii.*"

Both Dad'süren and Buyaa asserted that without *airag*, there can be no long-song. "It soothes the throat of a singer," Dad'süren told me, "and it gives the singer confidence to sing well." Buyaa added that the milk from the horse connects people with the livestock and with the land through the grasses that horse eats. That the horse's milk is collected with the aid of livestock-singing is another way in which the practice is linked to long-song in this region.

If spring is the season for *toiglokh*, fall is for long-song. Throughout the fall in Dundgovi, there are a number of *nair*, in which friends and family members gather in one person's home to feast, sing, and drink *airag*. Venerated singers, usually elderly men like Buyaa and Dad'süren, are called upon to begin and end these parties by singing long-song.

A *nair* is what Humphrey describes as a hospitality frame, a context for creating a tone of social equanimity. Legrain (2016) argues that the primary role of singing in the *nair* is to create a shared feeling to foster social cohesion. Madison Pískatá (2018) explains that long-song has a special power for encoding the affective character of a landscape (experienced through the reverberations of sounds across geological features) and reproducing it through performance. Good singing, as Dad'süren tells us, brings the vastness of the Gobi into the social space of the *nair*, just as good *toiglokh* brings the same peace to the mother sheep and lamb.

At the beginning of the fall, I returned to this rural county in Dundgovi for the first *nair* of the season. Silver bowl of *airag* in hand, Buyaa started out the celebration with "Kheer Khaltar." He had practiced a version of the song throughout the spring as *toiglokh*, so he was well prepared to perform the long-song version in this celebration. His sheep had become an audience for long-song, just as the sounds of what works to promote nursing found their way into his performance at this *nair*.

The main difference between this version of "Kheer Khaltar" and his *toiglokh* version was the addition of narrative, both textual and melodic. When singing to sheep, Buyaa used the words *"toig-uu toig-uu,"* which he explained have no meaning outside of their use for calming sheep. When singing the long-song, however, he performed a full set of lyrics: a poem that pairs the colors of different horses with moral instruction, exploring a realm of Dundgovi pastoral philosophy that is common for this genre.

The purpose of *toiglokh*, ultimately, is to induce the mother sheep to nurse and the new lamb to suckle. The singer stops whenever the relationship between the sheep is established. As such, livestock-singing rarely follows a melody directly from beginning to end. When singing to sheep, Buyaa broke into chant halfway through a verse, repeated sections of verses, and left melodic phrases unresolved. As a long-song song however, Buyaa performed "Kheer Khaltar" with more structure, tracing a melody that has specific beginnings and endings which break the text of the song into couplets.

Despite these differences, there were two key similarities between Buyaa's *toiglokh* and his long-song: style and purpose. The overall melody he sang and his placement and sound of ornamentations, the aspects of *urtyn duu* that vary greatly by singer and performance were the same as the version he uses for his nursing sheep. As he sang at this celebration, I heard him break into an extended falsetto improvisation in the second verse that I had heard him use for his sheep and goats several times during the spring.

Having practiced his songs in the pasture, Buyaa reflected on the tastes of his sheep to inform how he sang in this *nair*. He told me that, in both *toiglokh* and long-song, his goal is to create a calming atmosphere. Like

Dad'süren, he measures his skill as a singer against his ability to bring the same kind of calm to the sheep and humans alike.

Like a Lullaby

Why should singing to livestock cause them to nurse and, furthermore, to form an enduring maternal bond? Herders' opinions on why this practice works were mixed and varied from species to species. However, there were a few theories on the efficacy of nursing songs that applied to all five of the *tavan khoshuu mal* livestock animals.

One argument put forward by Buyaa is that the animals are trained from a young age to know that the song is a call to nurse, in the same way that they are trained to respond to a variety of herding calls. The other main theory, which Mandaa preferred, was that herders adapt sounds similar to those they hear from mother animals and consider the livestock's reactions as they produce these sounds. Taken together, these two ways of accounting for the efficacy of livestock-singing point to a coproduction of the practice and a mutual training, where herders teach animals how to consume a kind of music, just as the animals teach the herder how to sing it effectively.

Both of these perspectives depend on music's ability to relax the sheep and promote nursing. The empirical observations of my interlocutors present interesting contributions to recent studies in veterinary science on the use of music to relax domestic animals (Wells, Graham, and Hepper 2002; Kogan, Schoenfeld-Tacher, and Simon 2012; Snowdon, Teie, and Savage 2015) and to promote milk production among livestock (Uetake, Hurnik, and Johnson 1997). Both answers also point to ways for nonhuman animals to become critical consumers of human-produced music.

The first answer points to a way in which herders use *toiglokh* as a form of cross-species communication. As a form of training, *toiglokh* alters the social structure of the herd, putting the human in the role of most dominant member. However, it puts the herder in a unique position not just as a head of the flock, but as a facilitator of mother-child relationships as well. The herder draws upon long-song, a genre of music from a repertoire of human sociality, by incorporating the genre's melodies and vocal techniques as he performs *toiglokh* to promote this relationship between two sheep.

By combining forms of affective engagement from the human and nonhuman realms, the herder acts not as a sheep, but as what Despret would call a "human-with-sheep" engaged in a mutual transformation of identity across species (2004, 131). Just north of Mongolia, Willerslev (2007) describes contexts in which Yukaghir hunters in Siberia use aesthetic performance to bring the discrete worlds of human and elk closer together, with the goal of obtaining a kind of consent from the ungulate to hunt it. In a similar way, herders like Byambaa use the *toiglokh* song and accompanying ritual to bring the ontological categories of human and ungulate closer together.

The second answer, in which the herder learns what sounds to sing by imitating sheep, also highlights the permeability of the categories of human and nonhuman. The act of a nonhuman animal teaching music to a human creates a context in which both parties can cross the ontological boundary of species (Simonett 2015). The aesthetics that humans learn from performing *toiglokh* mingle with aesthetics they learn from the physical and moral character of the steppe and Gobi landscapes, forming the basis for their performance of long-song.

There was one other answer to the question of why *toiglokh* works that stood out to me for the connections between humans and animals it evoked. Ganbold, the former herder, now professional musician and music teacher, argued that the songs herders sing to nursing sheep have the same function as *büüvei*, a particular genre of lullaby for human children. In form, the practice is quite similar, as it involves the repetition of a single word, "*büüvei*," over the course of a semi-improvised melody to calm the child and make them sleep (see Dagvadorj 2016). While there is a commonly repeated etymology of the word as a contraction of "*büü ai*" ("do not be afraid"), in conversation, *büüvei* simply means "lullaby."

Ganbold explained that *toiglokh* and lullabies are both musical practices that develop attachment between a parent and child. Furthermore, for him, the two practices operate on similar theories of relationship building and character development. Returning to this practice often builds a feeling of trust in the child for the parent, and a connection between the two. He contended that this trust extends throughout the life of a person, setting them up to develop a *zöölön* or "softhearted" character rather than a *khatuu* or "hard" character that drives them to drink to excess, start fights, and cause trouble. Dagvadorj echoes these sentiments, writing that *büüvei* is as significant to a child's development as mother's milk, and that "of people with nasty personalities, we say: 'their mothers' must not have sung *büüvei* to them'" (2016, 3).

In Ganbold's view, *toiglokh* works the same way. The song, along with the caring embrace, creates a sense of trust in the young for the mother. It facilitates a mutual feeling of comfort and shared affection. Only in this construction, the herder acts as a surrogate. While sheep and lamb continue to build on this mother-child relationship, with all the care and trust that it involves, the herder's primary contribution to the development of that relationship, the *toiglokh* song, is temporary. Byambaa held the mother and child together in his embrace, and he created that relationship between the two, building their trust in one another while instilling trust for himself in both. His goal was to create the kind of mutual trust between the mother and newborn that would allow them both to reintegrate into the herd, at which point this kind of special care and attention would no longer be necessary.

Ganbold claimed that the social and moral aspect applies to sheep as well. Just as a lack of lullabies in childhood can lead a person down the path of becoming *khatuu* or "hard," neglected or abandoned livestock can grow up to be *zerleg*, "wild." He argued that an orphaned livestock animal lacks a necessary social relationship for its physical and emotional development, which, in turn, makes it unable to effectively socialize within the herd. A herder can heal this orphaned animal through *toiglokh*, instilling a *zöölön* character in the sheep, like a lullaby does for human children.

Each of these explanations relies on the idea that the performance of the music is acting upon the bodies of the sheep. The relaxation that the performance instills upon the body of the mother sheep then teaches the lamb and strengthens in the mother the autonomic response that this kind of singing means they can feel relaxed. In other words, all these explanations center affect, as the stimulus of the singing directly effects the bodies of the sheep and also leaves a trace of the context of the nursing ritual that will figure into the sheep's responses the next time they experience that same song.

Conclusion

The practice of *toiglokh* brings three different relationships into dialog with one another: human-sheep, sheep-sheep, and human-human. The first of these relationships is human-sheep, as the herder sings to the livestock and they respond by nursing. In Dundgovi, the herders I work with balance knowledge of *urtyn duu*, an aesthetic practice that works for fellow humans, with a careful consideration of the sheep's responses and the efficacy of *toiglokh*. Ideas and goals for the use of music in fostering a human child's social development and general positive sociality find their way into the act of caring for newborn livestock as well, rendering the act of livestock-singing something like a lullaby.

The second relationship involved in the practice of *toiglokh* is a sheep-sheep relationship. The herder works to develop a bond between the mother and the lamb that, if successful, will lead to an adoption and reintegration into the herd as a mother-child pair with the mutual acceptance that relationship entails. The trust and care of this relationship will continue to be a part of the emotional lives of the sheep and lamb long after the *toiglokh* is complete, and it will allow the orphaned or rejected lamb to take part in the social world of the herd. *Toiglokh*, then, is an important aspect of the maintenance of the herd's social cohesion, as it is threatened by the calamities of a dangerous birthing season.

The third type of relationship that intersects with *toiglokh* is human-human. Singing to sheep in the spring gives people opportunities to learn and practice their long-song techniques so that they can bring that experience into the *nair* during the fall and express the same kind of calm and comfort that they instill in the sheep with *toiglokh*. By combining the expertise gained through *toiglokh* with aesthetics drawn from landscapes, long-song singers bring a whole network of nonhuman pastoral relations into the *nair*.

Toiglokh has the ability to cross species boundaries because of its status as music, which Martinelli (2009) defines as "an affective, emotional engagement that is accessible to humans and non-human animals alike" (7). As Dad'süren explained, music gives us an opportunity to engage with the aesthetics and emotions of disparate entities. Humans can draw out the calming, expansive nature of the steppe landscape and use that to instill affective responses that will facilitate a mother-child relationship between two sheep. The herders I worked with take the sheep's responses to their singing into consideration as they perfect their long-song, treating the animals as a critical audience whose affective responses provide valuable information on the quality of their performance. Livestock-singing brings the worlds of sheep and steppe into the production of human cultural heritage, and human heritage becomes an active, vital aspect of those nonhuman worlds in return.

The herders that I worked with in Dundgovi recognized that people are interdependent with the nonhumans with whom they share an environment. As such, strengthening more-than-human relationships is a way to survive ecological crises, from the small-scale crisis of an individual mother camel rejecting her calf to the wide-ranging crisis of ecosystem breakdown. They conceptualized music and heritage as tools that had the capacity not only for building those relationships, but for repairing them when they have been harmed. The following chapter further explores the potential for musical heritage in repairing relationships between humans, horses, and the landscape.

CHAPTER 4

FOR THE HORSES

I returned to Ulaanbaatar from Dundgovi at the end of May to find that I had received an email from a friend, Chuluun, a retired chemical engineer and traditional music lover. The foaling season for the Mongolian wild horse, the *takhi* (*Equus ferus przewalskii*), was nearly over, he wrote. "I am going to bring a group of singers to them," the email said. "Would you like to join us as we sing a song for the horses?"

The *takhi* were once brought to the edge of extinction in the wild. By the end of the twentieth century, most *takhi* lived in zoos far from their historical territories. With the help of initiatives from zoos in central Europe, the Mongolian government has brought the *takhi* back to the Mongolian steppe. Chuluun is hopeful about the regeneration of this community of wild horses, but worried about their ability to adapt to life back in the wild.

Chuluun was raised in a family of nomadic pastoralists and horse racers. He spent his early years learning to train horses, to sing for horses as a form of encouragement, and to read the horses' reactions to see how they feel. Once he reached adulthood, Chuluun, like many Mongolians during the socialist period, left his family's nomadic pastoral encampment to work in the Eastern Bloc. He framed this plan to sing for the *takhi* at Hustai with a memory from those years:

When I was a little kid, I used to sing for the horses before races. The song gets the horses excited, so they jump and buck when they hear it. In 1982, I was in Bulgaria working as a chemical engineer. I missed my homeland and the steppe so much. My friend saw that I was sad and feeling homesick, so he took me to the zoo, to see the *takhi* they had there.

When I saw those horses, I was so sad. They were there in a pen. When I saw them, I felt like them. Like I was also in a big zoo. So, I sang a song for the horses. I thought, well, they are not in Mongolia but maybe it would be soothing to hear anyway. And when I sang for them, they pepped up! Started to jump and play and prance about.

Chuluun has relatively positive memories of the socialist period overall. He had a nice job, traveled often, and had a strong international group of friends. Despite all the reasons to be happy, he felt deeply sad during his time working in Bulgaria and could not articulate why. Seeing the *takhi* in the zoo was an awakening moment for him. The imperial project was, as he put it, a "big zoo." He was a living, feeling, conscious being, removed from his home in the steppe like the *takhi*.

This story had stuck with Chuluun for thirty-six years, still potent enough in his memory that his eyes misted up as he told it to me in the spring of 2018. By this point, he had retired from his career in engineering and had become a patron of the arts, especially long-song. Chuluun was happily back in the Mongolian steppe and had started taking as many trips to rural pastures as he could to be among the horses. The *takhi* were back in the steppe as well, after thirteen generations apart.

As he laid out his plan, Chuluun explained that he was nervous about the *takhi*'s ability to adapt to and thrive in their ancestral homeland. His concerns were exacerbated by the threat of climate change increasingly desertifying the ecosystems that *takhi* formerly roamed and increasing the severity of *zud*. In keeping with his singing to the *takhi* at the zoo many years earlier, he determined that the best way to welcome the horses back, to rebuild multispecies social relationships with them and help them integrate into the social ecology of the central Mongolian steppe, would be through traditional song.

Hearing the way Chuluun speaks about *takhi*, it is clear that he feels personal affection for them. As I described in chapter 3, Mongolian herders explicitly perform traditional songs for their livestock, so Chuluun and his team's act of singing to the *takhi* is a form of intimacy in this vein. In anthropological theories on domestic animals as kin (Haraway 2003; Govindrajan 2018; Schroer 2018) as well as theories on the human-animal relationship specific to transhuman pastoralism (Ingold 1988), the trust generated through acts of intimacy is weighed against acts of domination by the human over the animal. The *takhi* are not conventional companion species in Haraway's (2003) model, because they are not pets or domesticated livestock. Chuluun's relationship with the *takhi* may be generated through acts of intimacy, but domination is not an inherent aspect of his relationship to them.

The *takhi* are meant to be wild. The phrase "Przewalski Horses, the Last and Only Species of Wild Horse in the World" is blazoned on Hustai National Park's brochures and website (Хустайн байгалийн цогцолборт газар, n.d.). The Hustai *takhi* are highly dependent on humans, despite their wildness, staying close to the protection offered by the ecologists charged with studying them and surviving due to legal protections on their pastures. Fijn (2015) argues that *takhi* are wild not by virtue of their physiological condition, which has been actively managed by human zookeepers for at least thirteen generations between their capture and eventual rewilding, but according to their shy and distant disposition toward humans (294).

In *Shaving the Beasts*, John Hartigan (2020) found that wild horses in Spain had their own culture unto themselves, observable through bodily interactions between individuals within the herd. Likewise, the *takhi* have their own internal community structure and social world, the health of which is vital to the cohesion of their herds. Horses lead, follow, crowd, and make space for one another. They pay attention to one another and acknowledge the other's presence. They communicate and learn from one another. Though the animals are less intimately entangled with the humans they interact with than domestic livestock, by taking note of the patterns of these interactions a person can get a sense of the sociality of the herd.

Though wild animals have their own social worlds, it is vital to consider the effects that human activity can have on the social structure of nonhuman animals. When the Spanish wild horses in Hartigan's (2020) ethnography are rounded up once a year for a ceremonial shaving of their manes according to local tradition, the structure of their herds temporarily fall apart, before repairing themselves (10). This example demonstrates that the culture of nonhuman animals is simultaneously vulnerable to disturbance by interpellation in human social life, but also incredibly flexible and capable of recovery. Here in Mongolia, Chuluun is concerned with the *takhi*'s capacity to recover from not only social disruption, but exile from their home territories and near extinction.

Chuluun based his approach to establishing social relations with the *takhi* on his memory of intimate interactions with domestic horses in his youth. With those domestic horses, he reported having an easy time determining whether the animals trusted him or not; indeed, such trust was a necessary aspect of riding and racing them. However, the *takhi* are not quite domestic or totally wild. As such, developing relations with them carries both the familiarity of Chuluun's pastoral memories and the sheer ontological difference that can exist between a human and a wild beast of prey. More-than-human acts of intimacy can be fleeting and ambiguous as to the kinds of relation that they create.

The singers I profile in this chapter use musical heritage to try to create a horizontal relationship with the *takhi* that is intimate without involving the aspects of domination inherent to human relationships with domestic animals. Music is a more-than-human activity and can be used to create new kinds of affective relations between humans and nonhumans (Feld 1996; Martinelli 2009). By performing long-song to create a relationship with the rewilded *takhi* without the official support of Hustai National Park Trust, Chuluun demonstrates that cultural heritage, especially musical heritage, will be part of natural preservation projects whether officially sanctioned by the organization or not.

In this case, *takhi* act as bearers of a shared heritage, alongside their human counterparts. If, as I have maintained throughout this book, heritage is a distinctly neoliberal version of cultural beliefs and practices, then being a "heritage bearer" is a distinctly neoliberal form of social participation. As demonstrated in chapter 2, the transformation of a multispecies cultural practice like long-song into cultural heritage creates space for people to reshape modernist institutions to allow for more-than-human engagement. Through their performance of long-song for *takhi*, Chuluun and the singers involved in his project transform the *takhi* into heritage bearers. In doing so, they open the category of heritage bearer to include nonhumans.

This chapter describes the follow-up to a successful natural rejuvenation project, the repopulation of wild *takhi* horses in central Mongolia. Government and NGO-directed projects pick up on the division of heritage into natural, tangible, or intangible. Usually funding for these projects in Mongolia involves international monetary investment, which brings Western ideas about how heritage should be conserved. However, these divisions have not changed local ideas about the interdependence of natural and cultural heritage. When intangible aspects of heritage are not prioritized officially, people find ways to sneak cultural aspects into preservation efforts.

Chuluun's musical plan brings together natural and cultural heritage. Here is a case in which a natural heritage revitalization project does not in and of itself create public confidence in the long-term health of the animals, leading to a use of cultural heritage to create confidence in the project. Local people recognized that natural and cultural heritage cannot, or maybe should not, be managed without respect for one another.

The natural heritage program of reintroducing *takhi* to central Mongolia was successful in creating a healthy community of rewilded horses. However, Chuluun does not consider simply having healthy bodies to be the full extent of rehabilitating that community of wild horses. Because of the *takhi*'s long associations with humans, Chuluun considers the social relationship between humans and horses a necessary aspect to rebuild.

Chuluun chooses the cultural heritage practice of long-song to build connections with the *takhi* because he takes this form of traditional music as a more-than-human endeavor that has the potential for cross-species communication. In this chapter, I argue that the performance of cultural heritage is the method Chuluun and his team of singers used to build those multispecies relationships. This case offers a challenge to the distinction between environmental and cultural heritage and highlights the role that music can play in the mediating interspecies relationships involved in conservation.

Takhi

Takhi, also known as Przewalski's horses, are a wild relative of the domestic horse endemic to Mongolia and Xinjiang. They are often referred to in conservation documents as the world's "only" or "last" truly wild horses (Dulmaa and Shagdarsüren 1972) as opposed to feral communities of domesticated horses. They are diminutive and stocky, reaching only four feet high and around six feet from tip to tail, with thick necks and short legs. Unlike their domesticated cousins, *takhi* do not vary widely in coloration, being mostly dun with black manes, and a black stripe down the back, though subtle variations are identifiable.

The *takhi* were functionally extinct in the wild by the end of the 1960s. The degeneration of wild *takhi* populations and their preservation both began in the early 1900s. Reporting on the status of the *takhi* as of the mid-sixties, Mongolian ecologists Khaidav and Chagnaadorj (1969) reported that the number of wild *takhi* was falling due to what they referred to as "careless" hunting and *zud*, steppe winter calamities in which a season of drought is followed by heavy snow and make it difficult for ungulates to graze. Since then, a number of other theories have been put forward to explain how the numbers of *takhi* dwindled so severely. Explanations range from capture programs for Western zoos (Bouman and Bouman 1994; Van Dierendonck and Wallis de Vries 1996), competition for forage resources with livestock herds (Kaczensky et al. 2007), to military action in the *takhi*'s habitat along the Mongolia-China border between Khovd province and Xinjiang in the early twentieth century (Ryder 1993). A massive hunt ordered by the Qing emperor in 1750, resulting in the deaths of hundreds of horses, contributed to their decline (Mohr 1971). Broadly, most of the theories as to why the *takhi* died out in the wild agree that the cause was anthropogenic.

Commonly accepted theories on the extinction of the *takhi* present it as an inevitable result of increasing interaction with local people, placing much of the blame at the feet of local herders and subsistence hunters. Van Dierendonck and Wallis de Vries (1996) argue that the *takhi* were pushed to progressively less hospitable pastures by the nomadic pastoralists who had "colonized" the steppe over the course of several millennia (731). Interpretations of this sort that gesture widely to thousands of years of activities by "nomads" ignore the fact that, though there is a recorded history of local Mongolian interactions with *takhi* going back to the thirteenth century (Bökönyi 1974; Kahn and Cleaves 1998), the local population of *takhi* dropped significantly after World War II (Wakefield et al. 2002).

The most significant crisis within the *takhi* population takes place three decades deep into the Soviet reorganization of Mongolia and roughly fifty years after European capture programs had begun to disrupt wild herds and kill off adult *takhi* to bring foals back to zoos in the West. Though Van Dierendonck and Wallis de Vries (1996) do not agree that this is a primary cause of the *takhi*'s near extinction, they cite a personal communication with Mongolian scientist S. Dulamtseren who makes the claim that these Western zoo capture programs led to breakdown of internal social structures within *takhi* herds, seriously hampering their resilience and leading to their extinction. It is significant that the *takhi* began to die off at an increasing rate after European colonial activities in Mongolia at the beginning of the twentieth century and the introduction of Soviet modernity to Mongolia starting in the 1920s. Even operating under the flawed assumption that the final extinction of the *takhi* is simply the conclusion of a series of events put forth over millennia of competition between *takhi* and local herders, colonial modernity drove the *takhi* to extinction at an accelerated pace.

Sacrifice Species

In the mid-twentieth century, the *takhi*'s steppe cousins were also facing severe endangerment due to colonial modernization campaigns. At their height, *takhi* shared territory with saiga antelopes (*Saiga tatarica*) at the northern end of their historical range, and with musk deer (*Moschus moschiferus*) at the southern end. Each of these three ungulates are what I call sacrifice species for modernization campaigns.

Saiga antelopes are characterized by their upright, slightly spiral horns and pachyderm-like snouts. While the saiga's historical range spans from Mongolia to the Carpathians, the majority of the contemporary population are in Kazakhstan, with another population in Kalmykia and a separate subspecies in northern Mongolia (Bekenov, Grachev, and Milner-Gulland 1998). By 1950, they had only just started recovering from near extinction due to poaching when the USSR started using a significant portion their territory in the Kazakh steppe for nuclear testing (Kassenova 2022).

Musk deer historically live across Siberia, their territory spanning Russia, Mongolia, and China. They grow long, fang-like tusks rather than antlers. In the mid-1950s these creatures faced a crisis similar to that of the saiga antelopes. As part of China's Great Leap Forward, the state attempted to create self-sustaining musk deer farms by capturing and breeding wild deer to very limited success and leading to the animal's near extinction in the country (Chee 2021, 92–93). Like *takhi*, the musk deer did not do well in captivity and the disruption of their wild herds to replenish farm projects had a similarly devastating effect on their long-term herd health.

In each of these cases the ungulates were extracted or destroyed as part of a state's turn to modernize itself in the wake of World War II. Western Europe, the Soviet Union, and China treated the Central Asian steppe and Siberia as fringes that were full of extractable resources, both animal and mineral. These state powers saw the environmental effects on the steppe and the Indigenous people who lived there as justifiable in service of their modernization projects, marking the regions as "sacrifice zones" (Klinger 2017, 11).

As much as these areas were sacrifice zones, the *takhi*, saiga antelope, and musk deer that populated them were sacrifice species, whose lives and deaths were mobilized in the creation of modern environmental enterprises including industrial farms, zoos, and nuclear power. They remain sacrifice species to neoliberalism. Recently, they have suffered mass die-off events like the 2015 *Pasteurella multocida* outbreak among saiga antelope (Fereidouni et al. 2019) and the *zud* which led to breakdown of the Great Gobi B population of *takhi* in 2009–2010 brought on and exacerbated respectively by climate change.

Zoo capture programs were not the only projects through which European explorers and state representatives began to prospect on Mongolian territory at the beginning of the twentieth century. The management and extraction of wildlife resources falls into the same wave of institutional reordering of institutionalized music education and performance discussed in chapter 2. In the following chapters, musicians outline their experiences of the ongoing effects of the violence of Soviet colonialism. In a period of colonial violence affecting Mongolian people's lives, this community of endemic horses was also being subject to imperialism. The shared history of violence is not lost on people like Chuluun.

Preservation efforts for the *takhi* began in 1969 with a federal hunting ban, perhaps too little, too late (Dulmaa and Shagdarsüren 1972). It would not be until 1992, after the transition, that repopulation programs would be put in place. In cooperation with several European zoos and conservation NGOs, the Mongolian government has brought a total of eighty-four *takhi* from Western zoos to Mongolia during the period of 1992–2018. The Prague Zoo in particular, through their Save the Wild Horses program, has been an active partner with the Mongolian government, releasing breeding pairs of *takhi* and aiding them in acclimating to living wild on the steppe. Having taken a key role in the horses' extinction at the beginning of the century, Western zoos went on to become instrumental in the repopulation of the species at the end of it.

Hustai Nuruu National Park

The primary target area for these repopulation efforts has been Hustai Nuruu National Park* in Töv Province, central Mongolia (figure 4). Another population has been reintroduced to Great Gobi B Strictly Protected Area, split between Khovd province and Govi-Altai province in the southwestern Gobi bordering Xinjiang, one of the endemic habitats of previous *takhi* populations identified by Khaidav and Chagnaadorj (1969). While the Hustai population of *takhi* have been closely protected, staying in a national park where people are now barred from herding or hunting, the Great Gobi B population live alongside herders.

Hustai Nuruu, a fifty-thousand-hectare plot of land in the western Khentii Mountain escarpment just sixty miles west of the capital city, has emerged as the central area for repopulation programs. Because of its proximity to the capital city and the allure of seeing wild horses, Hustai is a regular destination for domestic and international tourists. Hustai is also central to Chuluun's story, as the spot that he chose to sing to the *takhi*.

The history of Hustai Nuruu is also the history of postsocialist nature preservation in Mongolia. In 1993, this area was designated a nature preserve for the primary purpose of reintroducing *takhi* to the wild and was upgraded to the designation of national park in 1998 (Хустайн байгалийн цогцолборт газар, n.d.). Hustai National Park Trust, established in 2003, was the first Mongolian NGO established to address issues of natural preservation. As of 2020, Hustai National Park Trust claims a population

---

* Also known as Khustain Nuruu, "Hustai Nuruu" is the conventional English spelling officially used by the park.

FIGURE 4 Takhi cross the road in Hustai Nuruu National Park. Photograph by K. G. Hutchins.

of 335 *takhi* in the park, making it the largest population of wild *takhi* in the world.

Other areas with significant wild *takhi* populations have not done as well. The previously flourishing community of *takhi* in Great Gobi B crashed during the winter of 2009–2010, due to a severe *zud*, which depleted *takhi* herds by 60 percent on average (Kaczensky et al. 2011). Compared to Hustai, nestled in the relatively temperate central part of the country and close enough to Ulaanbaatar to benefit from the resources the capital city can provide, Great Gobi B is in a remote location with a difficult climate.

Meanwhile *takhi* outside of the Central Asian steppe are also dwindling. Curiously, one of the most significant contemporary populations of wild *takhi* is a herd that has been living in the Chernobyl exclusion zone. The Ukrainian Askania-Nova nature reserve established a program to acclimate a herd of thirty-one *takhi* (twenty-eight from the reserve itself and three from a nearby stud farm) to be able to range freely in the exclusion zone (Zharkikh, Yasynetska, and Zvegintsova 2002). This herd has diminished from a healthy sixty-five horses down to around thirty as of 2011 and has likely continued to fall, due potentially to poaching and the resurgence of wild predators in the area (Gill 2018).

The Mongolian government considers the repopulation of *takhi* to Hustai as a successful endeavor so far. Furthermore, ecologists write that the reintroduced *takhi* have adapted well to life in Hustai, using available forage and resources in a similar manner as feral domestic horses, though staying close to their release sites (King 2002). The main unanswered question for Chuluun and many other local Mongolian people is, will the *takhi* be able to adapt to living life on the steppe after so many generations of living only in captivity? Chuluun maintains that there is more to living on the steppe than eating grass and finding potable water, even for horses.

There are two social relationships that are vital for the long-term survival of the *takhi*. The first is the internal social structure of the herds themselves. Social breakdown within herds was a major contributing factor in the species' first extinction (Bouman and Bouman 1994; Van Dierendonck and Wallis de Vries 1996, citing S. Dulamtseren). Scientists tracking the *takhi* population at Hustai pay close attention to how herds form socially as a measure of their adaptation to their new environment. This approach is standard among scientists tracking other populations, like those in Chernobyl as well (Zharkikh and Yasynetska 2009). While wild animals can repair their social structures after anthropogenic disruption on their own (Hartigan 2020), the scale of disruption that the *takhi* have faced leaves ecologists and other interested observers like Chuluun unsure if the horses can rebuild their band structure from scratch. The social structure of a herd is a difficult social relationship for humans like Chuluun to impact directly, though he still made an attempt.

The second social relationship at play is the relationship between *takhi* and local humans. This relationship is much more accessible to Chuluun and others like him who want to make sure that the *takhi* reacclimate to living alongside people successfully. To settle into the steppe, and become truly "wild," the *takhi* need to be able to take their role in relationship with humans again. While the Great Gobi B population of *takhi* live alongside herding families, the herds in Hustai live far away from humans, only seeing the scientists charged with tracking them and occasional tourists trying to get a glimpse of them through binoculars. To rebuild that social relationship, Chuluun devised a plan to sing long-song to the *takhi*, using cultural heritage to address what he saw as a potential problem for a natural heritage preservation project.

Chuluun saw a need to create a relationship with these horses. For him, this kind of multispecies entanglement was the only way to repair the damage done both to the horses and to him by the Big Zoo of European colonialism. To borrow a turn of phrase from Juno Parreñas (2018), Chuluun's project was an attempt to use cultural heritage to decolonize the extinction of the *takhi*.

Chuluun picked a critical time for the intergenerational survival of the *takhi* herd, foaling season, for this project. He assembled a team of singers that he had worked with in the past, a grandmother-daughter-granddaughter trio named Tsegii, Tsetseg, and Tungalag. A couple of days later, we piled into a Soviet-era Russian van and made the short trip from Ulaanbaatar to Hustai Nuruu National Park, ready to try singing for the wild horses.

To Hustai

When we first arrived in Hustai, we stopped just outside of the gates to the park for Tsegii and Tsetseg to make an offering to the land. They both flicked milk from measuring cups three times toward the valley that winds through the mountain range, a traditional spiritual practice called *tsatsal*. We waited for a bit on the outskirts of the park, in the hopes that the *takhi* would bring their newborn foals to water closer to evening. As we waited, the singers strategized on what songs to perform for the horses. Taking advice from Chuluun and the other singers, Tsegii took the lead and selected three songs from the canon of Mongolian traditional music, "Uyakhan Zambuu Tiviin Naran" ("The Sun Over the Placid World"), "Zeergenetiin Shil" ("Joint-Fir Hollow"), and "Tsombon Tuuraitai Khüren" ("Dark Brown Horse with the Rounded Hooves").

Each of these songs is a long-song, the semi-improvisational, highly melismatic genre of vocal performance discussed in chapter 3. Their first choice was "Uyakhan Zambuu Tiviin Naran," a song I was first taught by Dad'süren at that Dundgovi *nair* at the end of the summer. At the time, Dad'süren had said that the song draws heavily from Buddhist thought and expresses the interconnectedness of the lives of all the beings on Earth.

Tsegii explained that they chose this song as a way of establishing that all life is interdependent, including the lives of *takhi* and humans. A selection of the lyrics are as follows (table 1), with my translation into English.

"Zeergenetiin Shil" ("Joint-Fir Hollow"), is a song about the two protected hunting grounds of Chinggis Khan. Tsegii said that she chose that song because it is dedicated to wild game animals. She hoped that it would appeal to the *takhi*'s wild nature, and maybe give them more comfort in assuming the role of a newly rewilded population. The first four verses (table 2) also detail a perilous journey made by two horses.

TABLE 1 Selections from "Uyakhan Zambuu Tiviin Naran" in Mongolian and English

1. Жаа. Энэ сайхан замбуу тивийн наран Илхэн бүхий дэлхий дээгүүр Мөхдөлгүй дэлгэрч түгэн Мандаж мандсаар байдаг л билүү зээ, та мину зээ	1. Jaa. Beautiful sun over this gentle world will you always rise, above the entire planet spreading endlessly?
2. Жаа. Тэр лугаа адил Олон түмний минь өршөөл Үнэн сэтгэлтэй бүхнийг Ялгалгүй асарсаар байдаг л билүү зээ, та мину зээ	2. Jaa. The same way will my people care for others with compassion and an honest heart for all, without discrimination?
3. Жаа. Үүлэн чөлөөний наран мэт Өчүүхэн энэ явах насаа Үнэн мөнх дор барьж Үгүй муухайгаар хууртдаг шүү дээ, та мину зээ	3. Jaa. Like the sun freeing itself from the clouds, as you move through this humble life, hold on to the truth forever, do not be deceived by ugliness.
4. Жаа. Идэр цовоо саруул сэргэлэн насандаа Эс сурсан эрдэм номыг Өтөлж харьсан хойноо Эргэж сурна гэдэг маш бэрх биш үү дээ, та мину зээ	4. Jaa. In old age, looking back would knowledge left unstudied in the clear, energized years of youth be too hard to return to and learn now?

The opening four verses of "Zeergenetiin Shil" reflect on three worlds that horses can inhabit: wild, domestic, or lost. The wild deer are at home in the shrubland hollows. Likewise, the domestic sheep are in their place with the human herders among the encampments. The two roan horses, however, are lost, their place in the world uncertain. They have leagues to travel before they can leave the wilderness and rejoin their human companions.

The journey that these two roan horses take in the opening verses of the song is similar to the journey the *takhi* must take, but in reverse. The

TABLE 2 Selections from "Zeergenetiin Shil" in Mongolian and English

1.	1.
Зээргэнэтийн эхэн шилд	In the hollow where the joint-fir grows,
Зэрлэг буга урамдана	wild deer blow.
Зэрэгцээд ирэхийн үед	Approaching side-by-side,
Хоёр загал морь	two roan horses.
2.	2.
Алтай гэгчийн шилд	In the Altai hollow,
Арван буга дуудна	ten deer call out.
Адилтгаж ирэхэд минь	Approaching in step,
Аавын хоёр загал бий	father's two roan horses.
3.	3.
Хонин дундуур гарахад	Will our two yet reach us,
Хоёр загал морь гэнэ	across this empty banner?
Хошуу нутгаараа хөөсөн ч	Emerging from among the sheep,
Манай хоёрыг гүйцэх үү?	our two roan horses?
4.	4.
Айл дундуур гарахад	Will our two yet reach us,
Алдуул хоёр морь гэнэ	across this empty province?
Аймаг хотлоор хөөсөн ч	Emerging from among the
Манай хоёрыг гүйцэх үү?	encampments,
(Sampildendev and Yantskovskaya	our two lost horses?
1984)	

uncertainty in "Zeergenetiin Shil" is whether the horses will return to the herders' encampment and become domestic again. The *takhi* are lost, like the roans, but must escape the captivity of their zoo breeding and become wild once more.

When I asked why they chose "Tsombon Tuuraitai Khüren" ("The Dark Brown Horse with the Rounded Hooves"), at first Tsegii told me "it is a song about a little brown horse!" Then she followed up with "consider the lyrics." They go as follows (table 3), again with my translation.

TABLE 3 Selections from "Tsombon Tuuraitai Khüren" in Mongolian and English

1. Цомбон туурайтай хүрэн нь Цохилсон хар алхаатай Цовоо янзын Эгиймаа нь Цочоод сэрэхэд санагдлаа 2. Дунд ухаагийг эхэнд Дуутай мөндөр шаагина Дурсгал болсон Эгиймаагийн Дууг нь сонсоход содхондоо 3. Бараалан харагдах хөндий нь Байсан нутгийн бараа даа Багын амраг Эгиймааг Бараг нь хараад баясана даа 4. Нүүгээд явсан нутаг нь Нүүгэлтэж бараантаад харагдана Нүүдлийн хойноос харахад Нүдээр дүүрэн нулимстай 5. Ачаалаад явсан ачаа нь Арын замаар ганхана Ачааны хойноос харахад Алаг нүдэндээ нулимстай 6. Ооныхоёр эврийг Ороож зангидаж болддоггүй Орчлон хорвоогийн жамыг Огоорч мартаж болддоггүй	1. I wake up with a start, remembering clever, eager Egiimaa with her locks of black hair like the rippling mane of the dark brown horse with rounded hooves. Atop a small hill, loud hail falls. 2. I am struck when I hear the song that Egiimaa, now a memory, used to sing. 3. The valley that appears in the distance is a mirage of my old home. I would be filled with joy to see the distant silhouette of my first love Egiimaa. 4. The land where I have moved appears laid out in front of me. When I look back to where I came from, my eyes fill with tears. 5. The luggage I carry sways out along the northern road. When I look out behind the luggage my dark eyes tear up. 6. The two horns of the antelope can never come together and touch. The way of the world and of the universe can never be forgotten or denied.

There is a kind of grim humor in the choice of this song. In the lyrics, the narrator describes the pain of being forced to leave one's homeland. In the final verse, the narrator declares that there is no way to predict the future or to change fate. Taken together, the message that the singers attempted to convey to the *takhi* is clear: "We welcome you here as fellow living beings, we hope that you will become wild, but we understand that returning home is not the same as *being* home." In Dundgovi, Dad'süren had told me that it is normal for people to sing long-song to reflect on their own lives, contemplating their situation through the actions of the characters. Here Tsegii's choice of the songs reveal a subtle use of this logic, with messages that clearly use the plight of the *takhi* as an opportunity to reflect on the lives of the singers under postsocialism.

After dinner and a restroom break, we prepared to go. An unpaved dirt road winds through the valley of Hustai, eventually opening up to a few pathways leading to different areas of the park. On the road we passed a couple of cars coming back to the gate and asked them if they had seen any *takhi*, but they said that the horses were hiding on the far side of the mountain and would not come into view.

Discouraged by this news, we chatted to pass the time and keep up our spirits as we wound our way into the valley. Tsegii asked me if my research covered people singing to make it rain. I told her I had not seen any of that in person and asked her if she had. She had heard tales of things like that, but also had not experienced it in person. In fact, she told me, this kind of spiritual singing is relatively new for her.

Tsegii was born and raised in Ulaanbaatar. In her thirties she decided to learn long-song, but said she could never quite grasp that special essence that seemed to come naturally to the singers who grew up in the countryside—that is, until she moved to a provincial center to take a job as a banker and spent a couple of years seeing rural life.

Tsegii said that she knew she should figure out that missing element in her long-song. She described the way she taught herself long-song as a process of awakening an embodied, hereditary predisposition toward the music. "After all, it's in my blood," she explained, "I just had to activate that Mongolian sound with life on the rural steppe."

I present this quote in particular to highlight how Tsegii describes the relationship between her national identity and the cultural heritage of long-song as necessitating her embodied dwelling within the natural heritage of the rural steppe. This perspective draws on romantic nationalist

ideas about an atavistic relationship between the dominant national culture and the physical territory of the nation. This approach to national ideology that combines ancestry with landscape narratives is well researched
in the Mongolian context (see Bulag 1998).

However, Tsegii's quote is not simply a rote repetition of a nationalist
trope. Tsegii's recounting of the steppe was a story of what Ingold (2000)
calls a "dwelt-in world," in which humans and nonhumans co-constitute
each other through active engagement, or "dwelling" (5). In Ingold's construction, the landscape becomes a record of the lives dwelling upon it,
past and present (189). Tsegii framed herself as a person separated from
the steppe by the violent history of colonial modernization in Mongolia.
As such, dwelling in the steppe is a way for her to reclaim not only her
identity as a Mongolian person, but to reclaim the more-than-human
relationships that dwelling in the steppe entails. Learning long-song for
Tsegii meant creating relationships with nonhumans across the steppe
landscape, including animals and sacred mountains.

Tsegii takes the *takhi*, like her, as beings separated from the steppe by
a twentieth century history of violence. Taking the *takhi* as co-bearers of
heritage (national, cultural, and natural), she extends this embodied, national identity to the animals through her performance. In order to resume
their role as Mongolian wild horses, dwelling in the steppe, they must be
brought not just *back* to the steppe, but *into* a steppe that reverberates
with long-song.

We pulled up to the Hustai Park ecologists' station, a complex made of
a handful of felt round-tents outfitted with satellite and large antennae.
The scientists staying in the park to observe the *takhi* throughout foaling
season came out to tell us that the horses have been unusually nervous
around humans this year. They point us to where we might find some,
along a southern trail, but advise that we might not see any *takhi*, and
probably would not be seeing foals.

As we piled back into the van, Tsegii continued telling stories about her
journey as a long-song singer. Since coming into her own as a performer,
she told us that she had started having more run-ins with the supernatural.
She gave an example of a recent encounter she had with *lus savdag*, a kind
of nature spirit. Recently on a trip to perform in Bayankhongor, Tsetseg's
home province, Tsegii and Tsetseg passed a location where people usually

give offerings while traveling, a *joloochny ovoo* like the one I had just visited with Bayar a month earlier. Tsegii told us that they did not have any offerings, so they skipped it only to have their car break down a short while later. They managed to get to the next town and picked up a new car, but again neglected the offerings and again the car broke down. I asked if that spirit was tied to the road or to some kind of natural feature. She shrugged and said, "I have no idea, I just know it needed an offering."

This story points to Tsegii's continued process of using long-song as a way to access more-than-human relations on the steppe. She asked Chuluun and me what we thought of her story, if we believed that *lus savdag*, spirits of the water and land, could cause the problem and if they would lash out like that in response to a missed offering. Her story, and the lack of surety with which she told it, highlighted how ambiguous these more-than-human relationships can be, foreshadowing the difficulty we would have reading the responses of the *takhi* to Tsegii, Tsetseg, and Tungalag's singing later that day.

Chuluun, introspective, answered Tsegii's questions with a long story, which I had trouble following, about how *ovoo* worship contributes to bacteria transmission by bringing people together with spoiled food offerings. Tsegii rebuffed him, saying, "But our stomachs were fine, it's just our car that broke down, what's the cause of that?" He shrugged and joked, "Maybe you have a shitty car." We pulled over to the side of the road, ready to set up and wait for the *takhi* to come to us.

We set up around a spot where a little creek pools up into a pond, in the hopes that the *takhi* would come by to drink from it. Tsegii and Tsetseg pulled out their two-liter bottles of milk again and flicked spoonfuls of it in the four directions. It did not take long for little white spots to appear on a slope to our south. Chuluun pointed out the trajectory the horses seem to be taking, and we moved a little further down the road to avoid disturbing them or blocking their access to the creek. When the *takhi* came more clearly into view, I could see two white ones, a bay, and a black horse taking the lead, a surprising variety of colorations given everything I had read about the *takhi*'s uniform, dun appearance. Each of the horses in this first wave of *takhi* were about the same size, with no foals.

The three singers faced the horses and sang "Zeergenetiin Shil" together. The power of their voices carried across the valley to the *takhi*, and the horses immediately turned their heads toward the singers. They continued looking back at us periodically as they meandered toward the water. One, the bay, was so interested in us that he ended up being left behind and had to run to catch up with the rest of the herd. The ladies sang for about two minutes, stopping at the first stanza break after four lines.

The *takhi* approached the water as the singers switched to "Uyakhan Zambuu Tiviin Naran." Each time they sang, the three womens' voices echoed into the valley, though not simultaneously. Tsegii's voice led, at times driving ahead of the others, at times lagging, waiting for the others to catch up. When the herd disappeared fully behind a short hill over-looking the pond, the singers switched to "Tsombon Tuuraitai Khüren." This was the first long-song I myself had learned back in 2011 so, taken by the moment, I joined in the singing. Once our song ended, the *takhi* lost interest in us and made their way back into the valley.

From my perspective, it looked like the *takhi* had clearly come to listen to the singers and paid close attention to them. However, Tsegii seemed a bit crestfallen about the response by the *takhi*. As the *takhi* made their way back up to a sunny slope near whence they emerged and begin rolling play-fully in the dirt, she whispered, "They hardly noticed us at all." Grinning, she turned to Chuluun and joked, "Maybe you need to bring professional singers next time."

Chuluun had the sharp eyes of a herder, used to watching far-off ani-mals across the steppe. On a ridge far to the southwest he spotted two tiny flecks of white coming down the mountain, which turned out to be more *takhi*. Further investigation with the binoculars revealed three adult males with no foals, but we went to get a closer look just in case.

Across from them, on the northern ridge, we were able to spot mares with foals coming down for water. Though Tsegii seemed disappointed at the singers' efforts, Chuluun pointed to this emergence as a sign of success. "No matter what, we saw *takhi* and foals," he offered.

The *takhi* were not the only wild animals that came after the singing; on our way out we found a herd of thirty to forty deer had come down from the northern mountains to a slope overlooking the spot where Tsegii, Tsetseg, and Tungalag had been singing "Zeergenetiin Shil." Tsetseg qui-etly offered, "The song is for them, after all."

Conclusion

Compared to the surety of the socialist project, postsocialism in Mongolia is marked by ambivalent moments like these, where empirical projects designed ad hoc have confusing results. Was the singing successful in appealing to the *takhi*? Chuluun would say yes, but Tsegii was less sure. For both though, the next step was "come back and sing again." Connections like this need to be formed over time; there was never a doubt in the power of long-song itself in forging this interspecies connection.

In chapters 1 and 2, fiddlers like Ganbold and Ganaa maintained that horses had a vital role to play in the transmission of cultural heritage. However, in both examples, nonhuman animals are kept out of the very institutions charged with maintaining it. So, these fiddlers bring horses in at the margins of the institutions, practicing their long-songs in rural spaces during their conservatories' off-seasons.

Tsegii singing to the *takhi* is an intimate act. Chuluun conceptualizes it as a form of care, as the singing should help the horses feel at home on a once-lost homeland. However, the relationship built through these acts of intimacy is not necessarily meant to be kin or kin-like, as is the case with the kinds of nonhuman animals Haraway (2003) would call "companion species"—pets and domesticated livestock. Rather, the relationship is one of shared *nutag*, shared homeland, premised on the capacity of nonhuman animals to act as bearers of both natural and cultural heritage. This *nutag* relationship respects, even encourages, the wildness of the *takhi*.

In Hustai, the natural heritage project of rewilding the *takhi* herds shows the other side of the nature/culture split underlying international heritage politics. From Chuluun's perspective, the reintegration of the horses back into the steppe is missing an important aspect by neglecting the cultural aspect of their relationship with humans. So, he and Tsegii brought long-song in at the margins of this institution and sang for the horses. These cultural heritage bearers used traditional music to contribute to a natural preservation project. Chuluun and Tsegii's use of long-song to connect with repopulated wild *takhi* reentangles cultural and natural heritage. Furthermore, this performance explicitly positions *takhi* as heritage bearers, bound to the same embodied narratives as the performers themselves.

The future that Chuluun is working toward in this example is a multispecies future, premised as it is on the interdependence of humans and nonhuman animals for their mutual well-being. Furthermore, this is a more-than-human future, in that Chuluun and Tsegii frame their own well-being and the well-being of the *takhi* in terms of interdependence with the steppe itself. In the following chapters, I expand the frame of analysis to consider not only the roles of people and animals in cultural heritage, but those of the land, spirits, and other entities.

CHAPTER 5

WITH EACH PASS, ANOTHER STONE

When the fall semester of the Arts and Culture University started back up, I returned to Ulaanbaatar to continue working with urban-based musicians and heritage bearers. I stayed in a neighborhood colloquially known as Modny Khoyor, halfway up the hill leading to the Gandantegchinlen Monastery. Gandantegchinlen, known affectionately in the city by the nickname "Gandan," is a Gelug or "Yellow Hat" Tibetan Buddhist Monastery, one of the few religious institutions to survive Choibalsan's purges mostly intact. The area surrounding Gandan is something of a temple district, with smaller monasteries, religious schools, and Buddhist implement shops radiating out in a circle around it for several blocks.

One evening in winter I met up with a friend named Bayar at a South Korean chain coffee shop nestled between two monasteries in Modny Khoyor. Early in our conversation he told me a version of a story that I had heard a few times throughout the course of my research. A story about how people learned to live with mountains.

As the story goes, long in the past, people would unknowingly encamp near wrathful mountains. The mountains, offended by the humans' careless trespass, would bring down calamities upon them. So, the people put up *ovoo*, spiritually significant piles of stone, to identify these mountains and let others know the rules for engaging with them. I bring up this story not to assert a claim to origins, but to highlight the role of *ovoo* as advocates on behalf of humans. These ritually significant structures mediate the wills, needs, and behaviors of people and mountains to one another and thereby mediate conflicts between the two.

Ovoo are sacred heaps, usually made from piles of stone or collections of branches tied together by ritual sashes. Throughout Mongolia, many spiritually significant areas, especially mountains and major water features, are marked by *ovoo* of various sizes. A common form of worship at *ovoo* is to walk clockwise around the structure three times, picking up stones from the ground and tossing them on the pile as you make your silent circumambulation. Through this act, worshipping the mountain becomes a process of building the *ovoo* itself.

The *ovoo* works through accruing new stones, along with a variety of other offerings. Common offerings include teacups, Buddhist icons, horse skulls, and sashes. A comprehensive list of potential offerings is impossible, as people give offerings that represent their own personal needs. *Ovoo* also vary widely in terms of spiritual purpose, with specialized offerings to match.

Furthermore, ongoing debates of what are and are not appropriate offerings are themselves part of the *ovoo* tradition. Food offerings of milk, candy, or rice are especially contentious as they draw scavenging animals. Not all offerings are immediately physically evident, as musical performances are also common forms of *ovoo* worship.

Ovoo are constantly growing structures that bring together the wills of humans, sacred landscapes, and nonhuman animals and plants. Humans source the material to create and expand the pile from local nonhumans: trees, stones, and occasionally livestock. While people use the *ovoo* to commune with and ask for protection from mountains and lakes, nonhuman animals such as small rodents and birds make their homes in and atop the pile. An *ovoo* itself is a nonhuman with agency, directing people to worship in certain ways. However, these more-than-human interactions demonstrate that it is also a mediator for the agencies of nonhumans, overcoming ontological boundaries to communicate the wills of nonhuman animals, spirits, and geological features to humans.

In 2017, *ovoo* worship, included in a broad set of Mongolian land veneration traditions, was added to UNESCO's List of Intangible Cultural Heritage in Need of Urgent Safeguarding (UNESCO 2017). *Ovoo* also

figure prominently in the files detailing the cultural and spiritual importance of natural heritage inscribed on UNESCO's World Heritage List,
such as the "Orkhon Valley cultural landscape" (UNESCO 2004) and the
"Great Burkhan Khaldun mountain and its surrounding sacred landscape"
(UNESCO 2015a). These inclusions implicate *ovoo* in international politics
of heritage management and preservation. Handler (1988) contends that
heritage researchers objectify cultural processes through reporting on
them. As ethnomusicologist Jeff Todd Titon cautions, the politics of heritage can be used to transform cultural practices into exploitable resources
(2009, 9–10).

Above, I have presented generalized examples of the proper care and
management of *ovoo*. However, in practice, local people have different
ideas about their meanings and use. The inclusion of *ovoo* worship on an
international list of heritage exposes a wide field of place-based spiritual
practices and sacred locations to scrutiny from a global community of
heritage administrators and enthusiasts.

Local and international conflicts over *ovoo* are further complicated by
the material conditions and desires of the nonhumans involved. Beyond
being symbols, the sacred mountains and landscapes for which *ovoo* mediate are physical features housing multispecies ecosystems of plants and
animals. Furthermore, these geological features themselves actively participate in the social lives of the humans and animals residing upon them.

Ovoo operate in cyclical time in which eras repeat themselves like
seasons rather than finishing and fading into memory. No *ovoo* is ever
finished. People build them up over the course of repeated engagements
with the same landscape. Sometimes rocks fall from them, heavy winds
tear down branches that bear ritual sashes, or mice eat the food offerings
that make up the body of the *ovoo* and reduce its size. Then people slowly
build the *ovoo* back up as they continue to visit the same mountain pass.
Ovoo witness history in cyclical time as well. The purpose of *ovoo* in Bayar's
story is to remind people of past calamities to teach them how to account
for when those calamities come to pass again.

In this chapter, we will pass through three stories with the *ovoo* at the
center. Rather than taking a linear approach, I examine *ovoo* according
to their own rules, circling around each vignette to find the resonances
between them. First, I detail the experiences of a heritage bearer and
hunting guide, Bayar, to explore a case in which contestation on how best

to maintain an *ovoo* in an environmentally and spiritually sustainable way opens up a space for negotiations of eco-spiritual practice. Then I turn to the stories of two musicians involved in the heritage music industry in Ulaanbaatar, Tüvshee the horse fiddle player and Zulaa, a long-song singer, examining how they use *ovoo* to spiritually mitigate financial instability and avoid health crises. Finally, this chapter returns to Bayar to examine how *ovoo* spring up simultaneously as memorials of violence and caretakers of nonhumans in the form of ghosts and birds in the ruins of a monastery.

The people I profile in this chapter depend on heritage for their careers. Bayar draws on both natural and cultural heritage to support his income working as a tour and hunting guide. Operating out of Ulaanbaatar, he spends the summer traveling to a variety of natural heritage zones throughout rural Mongolia, such as Great Burkhan Khaldun Mountain and the Orkhon Valley. He draws on his upbringing in a herding and hunting family in rural northern Mongolia to inform how he engages with these landscapes, trying to mitigate the spiritual and ecological harm of international tourism on these sites.

Tüvshee returns in this chapter. He is a horse fiddle performer and teacher, and as such, heritage is at the core of his career. The privatization of Mongolia's economy has made it so that working as a musician is not enough to support a family, so he started a side business selling electronics, based on the knowledge he gained experimenting with blending horse fiddle and electronic music in the 1990s. Zulaa is a long-song singer, and recent Arts and Culture University graduate. At the time of my interview, she was not employed consistently by an orchestra or conservatory. Both Tüvshee and Zulaa performed long-song to sacred mountains around Ulaanbaatar to ask for career opportunities and good fortune.

Natural, Tangible, and Intangible Heritage

UNESCO maintains distinct lists for identifying different types of heritage, originally dividing the concept into "natural heritage," socially significant and unique environmental zones, and "cultural heritage," architectural monuments of social and historical significance (UNESCO 1972). Throughout the 1980s and 1990s, representatives from nations in the global south advocated for UNESCO to consider intangible forms of cultural heritage as just as vital and meaningful as artifacts of physical culture, critiquing the Eurocentrism of conceptualizing culture primarily in terms of architecture (Bortolotto 2006). The actions of these representatives lead to what Bortolotto (2006) describes as an increasing shift toward thinking of culture in terms of ongoing processes rather than fixed objects. As a result of this shift, in the early 2000s UNESCO broke down the category of cultural heritage into two further subcategories: "tangible" heritage, in the form of culturally significant artifacts and architectural sites, and "intangible" heritage, referring to practices, beliefs, and knowledge maintained through oral history (UNESCO 2003).

UNESCO (2018) further breaks down the category of intangible cultural heritage, maintaining two distinct lists: the Representative List of the Intangible Cultural Heritage of Humanity and the List of Intangible Cultural Heritage in Need of Urgent Safeguarding. The Representative List serves to increase the global visibility of local practices that demonstrate the diversity of human culture. Meanwhile the List of Intangible Cultural Heritage in Need of Urgent Safeguarding identifies those cultural practices that are in immediate danger of disappearing due to external factors.

In practical terms, inclusion in the latter list also includes measures to aid local people in the performance and transmission of their heritage. Many Mongolian traditional practices are closely tied to nomadic pastoralism, which is threatened by both environmental degradation due to climate change and the neoliberalization of Mongolia's economy. As such, most of the cultural practices I describe in this book are covered under List of Intangible Cultural Heritage in Need of Urgent Safeguarding.

Anthropologists have questioned the validity of separating "natural" from "cultural" phenomena (Strathern 1980; Descola and Sahlins 2014). The elements on the natural heritage list have value as heritage by virtue of human interactions with the environment and efforts to imbue it with meaning (Cleere 2001; Kirshenblatt-Gimblett 2004). Tangible heritage consists of objects that have no inherent meaning or cultural value outside of the intangible heritage to which they are connected (Byrne 2009). By the same token, the intangible aspects of social lives are inextricably embodied through and constrained by the material reality of heritage bearers' lives (Kirshenblatt-Gimblett 2004; Dirksen 2019).

The interdependence of natural, intangible, and tangible heritage is especially clear in Mongolia, where places like Great Burkhan Khaldun mountain are added to the world natural heritage list because of their role in mountain worship, with *ovoo* listed as the site's culturally significant architecture (UNESCO 2015a). *Ovoo* highlight how permeable and inter-related these categories truly are. They are artifacts of tangible heritage that accrue more artifacts in the form of offerings of ritual sashes, ceramic icons, horse skulls, and the like. They mark areas of ecological and cultural significance such as sacred mountains and lakes that are home to spirits, where social and environmental prominence are inextricably intertwined.

Heritage and Conflict

State powers can mobilize cultural heritage to ratify national boundaries and disempower minority voices (Handler 1988). The ruling party of the Mongolian People's Republic did something like this in the twentieth century when they elevated the Khalkha ethnic majority's traditions to the status of national culture (Bulag 1998). However, heritage also forms the core of counter-hegemonic histories that oppressed people can use to appeal to the international community and subvert elite and national-istic narratives (Graham 2002; De Cesari 2010; Camal 2015). On a more fundamental level, designation and consumption of heritage can be de-scribed as a measure to combat the social effects of neoliberalism, as peo-ple transform lifeways that are incompatible with global capitalism into consumable aspects of a tourist economy (Kirshenblatt-Gimblett 1995; Lowenthal 1996).

Each of these arguments foregrounds human contestations and nation-alist politics involved in heritage-making. However, a variety of nonhu-mans are also central to discourses on heritage within Mongolia, from the living plants and wildlife of natural heritage zones to the mountains and spirits that populate culturally significant places and practices. Following the recent turn in anthropological literature that considers the sociality of nonhumans (Van Dooren and Bird Rose 2012; Tsing 2013; Posthumus 2018) and their role in negotiations of power (Povinelli 2016; Govindrajan 2018), I take nonhumans as actors in contestations over heritage. I am drawn to wonder what role nonhuman animals, spirits, and landscape features have in these conflicts.

The designation of spiritual practices and sacred sites as heritage opens up local practitioners to international scrutiny. Inclusion in UNESCO's heritage lists requires long applications which are reviewed by committees to determine whether a practice is unique to the region and of global cultural value. Even after a successful inscription, practitioners are subjected to the informal but high-stakes scrutiny of tourists' expectations. Tourists bring ideas about what "authentic" Indigenous artistic practices should look and sound like, influenced by their desire to escape the disenchantment of neoliberal modernity (Rees 1998). For the heritage bearers I interviewed, this external scrutiny led to unavoidable conflicts. However, in each of the cases I outline below, these heritage bearers settle the conflicts through the maintenance of *ovoo*. Through cleaning, building, and performing for *ovoo*, they access the more-than-human network of animals, spirits, and geological bodies that destabilize the colonial impositions of European heritage politics.

I take *ovoo* as what Latour refers to as "mediators," entities that transmit force or meaning between actors (2005, 39). The *ovoo* carries offerings from humans to the spirits of the mountain and transmits the protection from those spirits back to the humans. Engagements with earth-based spirits, much like engagements with wild animals as seen in the previous chapter, often lead to vague, contradictory, or difficult-to-read responses.

Bayar asks for protection and forgiveness from the land by adding stones and clearing off food offerings from an *ovoo*, making it larger and changing its material components in the process. As it becomes larger, the *ovoo*'s prominence against the backdrop of the local landscape grows, increasing its potential to be seen across the steppe and incorporated into future rituals.

This chapter explores three sites of conflict over the practice and administration of heritage in which *ovoo* play central roles. In the following cases, *ovoo* create, prevent, or resolve disharmony through their presence and growth. *Ovoo* are nonhuman mediators capable of transmitting meaning between humans, animals, mountains, and spirits across a network in which their worlds are mutually intelligible.

By taking a multispecies approach to my examination of *ovoo* practices, I highlight the full range of actors involved in the shaping of heritage, including those nonhumans left ignored by readings of heritage that focus solely on conflict between humans. I argue that the role that *ovoo* play in these conflicts demonstrates that collaborations with a broad, interconnected field of nonhumans is central to how people mobilize heritage and will be a vital part of its preservation whether or not this relationship is intentionally fostered at the institutional level.

First Pass—The Tour Guide Pilgrimages

Bayar is a storyteller, a spiritualist, and ethnographer. At the time of this interview, Bayar had just returned from a summer spent working as a tour guide for Westerners looking for a rural adventure. During the summers, Bayar is a sought-after guide, especially with big game hunters. This is due in part to his proficiency in English and experience with Americans, but also because of his role as a heritage bearer along with his intimate knowledge of Mongolian landscapes and wild animals. He told me the story that begins this chapter as a way of introducing his approach to working as a guide. He expanded on the legend:

> Each mountain has different rules for how to interact with it. So people put up *ovoo* at different parts of the mountain to make those rules known. An *ovoo* teaches you how to interact with the mountain. One might be set up to mean "adults only past this point," or another might indicate "men go up this path and women around to that path." But they always tell you "approach with reverence."

As part of his explanation of the history and folklore of *ovoo*, Bayar mentioned that *ovoo* worship is central to his spiritual practice. He told me that he worships nature in a way that he referred to as "sort of shamanic." As Bayar put it, "My grandmother and great-grandfather were shamans, and they taught me all about worshipping nature. They taught me how to respect the land." He clarified quickly that he did not consider himself a shaman, but that he sees things in a shamanic way based on veneration of the sky, the land, and nonhuman animals.

When I asked him to elaborate on what seeing in a shamanic way meant, he responded, "See, shamanism is empirical. You see it, you believe it. Religion requires too much imagination. You white people are very imaginative. When you look up, you look beyond the sky, and imagine a god out there in a whole other world. When I look at the sky, I just see the sky."

Bayar is Buryat, a member of an ethnic minority group that was the primary target of Stalinist purges in Mongolia during the 1930s and '40s. The state ban on religion in both Mongolia and the Soviet Union along with the targeted state violence against the Buryat community have resulted in a significant disconnect between humans and spirits for many contemporary practitioners of Buryat shamanism. Manduhai Buyandelger (2013) argues that the primary way that Buryat shamans repair the damage to people's relationships with spirits and recover from the histories of violence that come with it is through acts of remembering. Shamans mediate these rituals of remembering, acting as the conduit through which spirits can communicate with people directly. Bayar is not a shaman, but he places himself adjacent to that tradition. The mediator he relies on is the *ovoo*.

Bayar is proud of his ability to read the land and the behaviors of wild animals, skills he attributed to the knowledge passed down from his shaman grandmother and his subsistence-hunter grandfather, respectively. However, he made it clear that he cannot commune with those nonhumans directly. He makes his prayers silently to himself as he passes around *ovoo*, using it as an intermediary that will pass his prayers on to the sky, the mountain, and the animals.

Bayar's role as an intangible heritage bearer affords him both social and economic capital within the rapidly expanding tourism industry in Mongolia. Tourism, especially trophy hunting, offers him opportunities to pursue lucrative side gigs throughout the summer. However, he reported ambivalent feelings about this line of work. "On the one hand," he told me, "it is pretty ridiculous that people come to Mongolia just to kill a ram." Bayar mentioned that some hunters from the United States and Europe even spend tens of thousands of dollars on permits to try to shoot endangered endemic Mongolian animals. "They don't even pay by the animal, just by the bullet. One shot, if they miss, it's over."[*]

---

[*] In his 2019 article on Donald Trump Jr.'s trophy hunting scandal, Anand Tumurtogoo estimates that western trophy hunters spend $20,000–50,000 apiece on

UNESCO (1972) identifies the presence of threatened or endangered animals as a significant element of natural heritage. If endangered game animals like the Altai argali ram (*Ovis ammon ammon*) constitute a fundamental resource for Mongolia's natural heritage areas, then international trophy hunting is a form of natural heritage consumption. This corner of the heritage industry is especially troubling for Bayar, having been raised in a subsistence-hunting family whose spiritual practice involves veneration for sacred game. Still, he decided that if he is part of the hunt, he can keep the damage the hunters make to the environment and to the wild flocks to a minimum. As he put it, "I lead the hunters to old or sick animals, never to mothers. And I make the necessary prayers."

Bayar explained that his travels around the country as a tour and hunting guide to natural sacred spaces give him the opportunity to tend to these landscapes as a form of spiritual work. As he described, both international and domestic tourism put physical and spiritual burdens on the landscape. He said that foreign trophy hunters cause obvious problems for wild animals, disrupting the social structures of their flocks by carelessly targeting according to size and accessibility rather than hunting in an informed, ecologically beneficial manner. He pointed out that even supposedly nonviolent eco-tourism disturbs wild animals and plant life, as people trample wild forage and leave plastic litter behind.

Bayar is continually faced with the question of how to address those damages and mitigate the spiritual impact of his own role in it. He concluded that he could lessen the physical and spiritual damage to wild flocks and herds by directing hunters to appropriate game and making his prayers via local *ovoo*. Often, these prayers involve cleaning away litter from the *ovoo* as well.

The spiritual practices Bayar described involved some socially risky behaviors. "Not everyone agrees on my definition of litter," he explained. Some of the things he clears away are widely accepted to be litter, things like cigarette butts or plastic water bottles. However, he also clears the food offerings from *ovoo* and cuts the ritual sashes from saplings to allow them freedom to grow. I asked if the spirits of the land might be offended

permits to go on hunting tours in Mongolia, targeting endangered wild game like argali rams.

by his removal of their offerings. He told me that practicing his religion means he must keep the *ovoo* and the ecosystem healthy.

"The food draws rodents," Bayar explained, "who live inside the *ovoo*, and infest it with their nests." The rodents would then take these offerings as their own, gnawing away at the innards of the *ovoo*. He described in great detail how rodents knock over the carefully placed ceramic offerings and disperse piles of burning incense with their crawling bodies. These rodents have their own relationships with the *ovoo* in which they dwell. It protects them and provides them with food and shelter. However, their patronage of the *ovoo* is at odds with Bayar's, undermining its structural integrity and bodily purity.

Even though he means well, Bayar admitted that this practice occasionally gets him in trouble with local people. On his most recent trip through the Khangai mountains, his *ovoo* maintenance activities caught the ire of a local herder, who caught Bayar removing offerings. "I was throwing away rice and candy that had been left on the *ovoo* and I heard this guy shouting at me!" He laughed as he told this story of how he found himself involved in a three-way struggle between himself, the herder, and a colony of mice. Bayar and this herder, whose name he never mentioned, argued over this issue for some time. Bayar acted out the confrontation: "The herder said, 'What are you doing with my offerings? Don't you respect the *ovoo*?' I told him, I respect the *ovoo*, that's why I'm doing this!" As he told the story, his voice became louder and his gestures more animated, drawing attention from the other coffee shop patrons. He smiled and sheepishly added, "See? Troublemaker."

Though the argument started contentiously, their shared goal of creating and maintaining a healthy spiritual landscape through proper care of its *ovoo* allowed them to end the conversation amicably. Bayar continued his story quietly. "I let him explain his viewpoint to me, and then I explained to him how I see the world. I told the guy that we have to adapt our thinking because the environment is being destroyed too fast these days and we have to be really careful with how we manage these sacred landscapes." In the end, they compromised. The herder conceded that Bayar might have some insight from his experiences in a wide variety of sacred spaces, while Bayar admitted that he should show more humility toward local stewards of the land. The herder agreed to let Bayar finish clearing off the *ovoo* so long as he made an offering of his own, in his own way. He set up a wooden post to adorn with the ritual sashes he had cut from nearby saplings. The foreign tourists that Bayar was working for at the time sat awkwardly in the van, with no knowledge of the Mongolian language, and thus not privy to the conversation.

Working as a tour guide presented Bayar with an internal conundrum. He balanced his displeasure at participating in a tourism industry that exploits the landscapes he holds sacred against the idea that this line of work might be the best opportunity to mitigate the spiritual and ecological damage that industry creates. He resolved this dilemma through his maintenance of the *ovoo* he finds around tourist destinations. *Ovoo* offer him an opportunity for some spiritual and cultural resiliency within the broader apparatus of tourism that heritage creates. However, his strategies for tending them have brought him into external conflicts with local people and nonhuman animals.

Second Pass—Music for the Mountain

The designation of *ovoo* as Mongolian cultural heritage opens local people's interactions up to critical consumption by outsiders, particularly Western cultural tourists. In this section, I present cases where Mongolian artists use traditional music as a spiritual practice dedicated to *ovoo*. I further examine how the designation of *ovoo* as heritage leads to pushback on Mongolian musicians' personal religious practices from Western observers.

I spent the winter of 2017 in Ulaanbaatar, working with horse fiddle performers and instructors like Tüvshee, who specializes in long-song. In my interview with Tüvshee, I started out with questions focused on the economic aspects of the heritage music industry. Before long, he stopped me, saying "you cannot really make a living selling traditional music, not in Ulaanbaatar." He crossed his arms over his chest and continued, "I mean think about it, in Mongolia we only have a population of three million people. Even if every person in the country was my fan, I would have a hard time making ends meet just selling albums." In fact, though he is a professional horse fiddle performer, composer, and professor, his main source of income is an electronics business that he runs on the side. Many of the traditional musicians and artists I interviewed that winter were in a

FIGURE 5 View of Ulaanbaatar from Zaisan Monument, the entry point to Bogd Khan. Photograph by K. G. Hutchins.

similar situation, balancing an unstable and underpaying career in the arts with other business pursuits that offer more financial security.

Tüvshee finished his explanation of the grim realities of the Mongolian traditional music industry with this concession: "Playing the fiddle does help me make money though, in a way." When he has a financial concern, he said that he bundles up his fiddle, hikes up to one of the sacred mountains that ring the city, and plays long-song to the *ovoo* there as a way of asking the spirits of the mountain* and its rivers** to help him in business.

Ulaanbaatar sits in a bowl formed by four holy mountains: Bogd Khan, Chingeltei Khairkhan, Bayanzürkh, and Songino Khairkhan. Most prominent among them is Bogd Khan, which sits at the south

---

* *Savdag*, mountain spirit.

** *Lus*, water spirit.

end of town (figure 5). It is one of those underrepresented places in the history of natural heritage management, established as a nationally protected natural area by the Mongolian government in 1778 (Atwood 2004; UNESCO 2015b) predating the 1872 formation of Yellowstone Park by nearly a century. In addition to being a national park, Bogd Khan, along with the other three mountains that ring the city, is a major part of the spiritual character of Ulaanbaatar. As with other natural heritage areas throughout Mongolia, communities of nonhuman animals make up the spiritual landscape of Ulaanbaatar's holy mountains. Bogd Khan in particular is known for its elk, and protection for the wild game has been a major part of natural preservation laws of the site since the eighteenth century (Atwood 2004).

Tüvshee broke down for me the way he prays to these mountains, explaining that the wood and rosin that go into the performance of the fiddle create a sympathetic relationship between the music of the fiddle and the spirits of landscape. The horsehair from the instrument's strings brings the nonhuman animals who live on the mountain into this relationship as well. He said that he taps into that connection to communicate his needs and his feelings to the otherwise unreachable mountain. In this ritual, the horse fiddle and *ovoo* are his mediators. "This is the primary way I practice my religion," he explained.

Unlike Bayar, Tüvshee did not describe himself as shamanic, nor did he describe himself as worshipping nature. He is a devout, practicing Buddhist. I bring this fact up only to highlight that *ovoo* practices are not necessarily tied to one religion or philosophy in the Mongolian context. Rather, *ovoo* worship is tied to a discrete set of social relationships between particular people, mountains, spirits, and animals.

Using musical performance as a form of worship or veneration of mountains and water features is a well-documented aspect of rural spirituality in Mongolia (Pegg 2001). Outside of Mongolia, the practice of making musical offerings to land-dwelling spirits is widespread throughout nomadic Inner Asia as well (Levin and Süzükei 2006). Tüvshee brings this practice to the distinctly urban setting of Ulaanbaatar's Bogd Khan Mountain.

Bogd Khan Mountain is one of the few sacred natural spaces in Mongolia to have a centuries-long history as a fixture of a major city, seeing the rise of Khüree and its eventual transformation into Ulaanbaatar (Atwood 2004). Tüvshee's interaction with Bogd Khan as a protector takes a distinctly urban form. In addition to asking for financial stability, he told me that he conducts this ritual at the beginning of winter to protect him from air pollution-related illness and car accidents, two major physical dangers of Ulaanbaatar life.

Tüvshee's comments about the close connection between long-song, *ovoo*, and urban life stuck with me throughout the rest of that winter. A few weeks later, over coffee with a group of friends, I asked Zulaa, a professional long-song singer, what she thought about the relationship between music and Ulaanbaatar's sacred mountains. She told me she goes up Bogd Khan Mountain once a week in the winter. Hiking is important for her lungs and voice, especially during this season when air pollution is at its worst. Born and raised in Ulaanbaatar, she finds the clear air of Bogd Khan a relief. Madison Pískatá (2021a) argues that this way of engaging with Bogd Khan demonstrates the mountain's agentive ability to compel humans to worshipful action. The presence of Bogd Khan traps smog in the city, and so is the spiritual being with the power to offer respite from that pollution.

Though Zulaa usually likes the company of the hiking groups, she said that she goes up alone on the days leading up to a major performance. She has a ritual for those occasions, in which she lugs a massive backpack up the mountain trail. Upon reaching a flat peak ringed by *ovoo* of different sizes and ages, she stops and sets down her pack. Carefully, meaningfully, she removes a bundle, which she unrolls into a performance *deel* and set of horn-style hair plaits. She sings to the Bogd Khan in full performance dress, to ask the mountain to help her in her upcoming performances and send some financial opportunities her way. With New Year's celebrations and the threat of family hospital bills, winter is always a financially difficult time of year for Ulaanbaatarites.

Zulaa makes her living as a professional singer and is a member of the Mongolian National Long-Song Association, but at the time of this conversation she did not have a consistent appointment in an orchestra or ensemble. She mentioned that she had a featured performance coming up. So, she would visit Bogd Khan soon and perform the songs she was planning to sing for it. She would use this performance as an offering to the mountain and ask for her concert to go well and lead to more consistent employment or even to a record deal in return.

As she recounted this story, one of our mutual friends was steaming. Carl, a European expatriate, long-term Ulaanbaatar resident, and self-styled expert on Mongolian traditional music, reacted to Zulaa's story hotly. Rolling his eyes, he berated her: "Asking for money? This is a perversion of the traditional way." Carl had positioned Zulaa within the savage slot, the ever-shifting category of non-Western people which the Western capitalist imagination self-defines against (Trouillot 2003). In Carl's imaginary, Zulaa, being an Asian traditional musician, should occupy a utopia that is entirely outside of capitalism and modernity. There is considerable pressure for Indigenous musicians in Asia to perform primordialism to match outside consumers' expectations of "authentic" cultural heritage (Rees 1998; Wong 2019). In Zulaa's case, this pressure extends to her personal life as well, as Carl expects her to live her entire life entirely outside of neoliberalism with no need for money.

Both long-song and ritual practices of worship at *ovoo* are part of Mongolia's internationally recognized intangible cultural heritage. Zulaa's appeal to *ovoo* and private mobilization of intangible cultural heritage practices to meet financial needs offended Carl's sensibilities. Based on Orientalist ideas about authenticity in Indigenous Asian intangible heritage, he argued that *ovoo* should not be used with material ends in mind. In response to Carl's outburst, Zulaa put up her hands. She pointed out that, though tradition is fine, "no one can survive trying to live an ancient life in the modern day."

Zulaa and Tüvshee both use long-song to appeal to mountains, via their *ovoo*. Mountains then intervene on their behalf, helping them navigate the inherently cosmopolitan calamities of Ulaanbaatar life, from financial insecurity to increasingly severe climate disasters and their consequent health crises. In this ritual, the *ovoo* act as mediators as they carry Tüvshee and Zulaa's offerings to the mountain and direct the mountain's power back in turn.

Though both Zulaa and Tüvshee were very open about the fact that they perform music at *ovoo* as a way of venerating local mountains, they kept many details about these performances private. They declined to specify what songs they chose or how they chose them and what aesthetic choices informed their performances. In both cases, the idea of me coming along for one of these performances was out of the question. Though neither said as much, I inferred that they were comfortable with opening only some aspects of *ovoo* worship to outside scrutiny.

Zulaa and Tüvshee's usage of a heritage music and mountain-worshipping rituals, both of which have been designated intangible cultural heritage by UNESCO, to resolve distinctly modern, urban issues leads to a secondary conflict. The inscription of these concepts as heritage creates a cosmopolitan consumer base, who bring with them Western notions of what is an appropriate approach to traditional spiritual practices. The *ovoo* for better or worse, with its premodern history and ancient appearance, was the centerpiece on Carl's reprobation of Zulaa. It was the fulcrum around which broader conflicts of colonialism, race, and gender played out between friends at a coffee shop downtown.

Final Pass—Monastery Ruins

At the end of the following spring, I joined up with Bayar again. The tourist season was about to pick back up, so he wanted to revisit some spots in the Gobi, monasteries mostly, to scope them out for future tours. I went with him, taking this as an opportunity to see the back end of the tourism industry.

We started our journey in the typical way for those leaving Ulaanbaatar and heading into the country: with an offering to a *joloochny ovoo*, a drivers' cairn. Bayar took his time clearing off food and drink offerings. He showed me a bottle of vodka that he had pulled off the *ovoo* before tossing it in the trash can. Grimacing, he shook his head and we took to the road.

Of the monasteries we visited throughout the Gobi, one stood out in particular for the more-than-human network it brought together. Süm Khökh Bürd is both the ruin of an ancient monastery and an oasis that gives migrating birds a place to rest. The small wetland surrounding Khökh Bürd was breathtaking, cut as a band of greenish-blue water and tall, waving yellow reeds against the red and brown backdrop of the semi-arid steppe (figure 6).

As the length and severity of droughts in the region become worse in response to climate change, water features like this one are becoming more vital to the birds who migrate through. Not far away in this same province was the dried up lake I had visited with Myagmar. Approaching Khökh

FIGURE 6 Süm Khökh Bürd and its surrounding wetland. Photograph by K. G. Hutchins.

Bürd, both Bayar and I were shocked to see flocks of ducks and seagulls. Just under the shadow of the nearby *ovoo*, a nesting pair of demoiselle cranes pranced in the shallow, slowly coursing water.

Before entering the monastery, we visited the *ovoo* on the overlooking hill. From this vantage point, we could clearly see ruins poking up from behind the reeds. Bayar directed my attention to a single swan sitting regally among the rushes in the heart of the marsh, flanked by a dozen seagulls, a few ducks, and two cranes. He told me the swan was a sign that the *ovoo* around the wetlands were doing good work, indicating that some of their duties were to sufficiently maintain the health of the wetland so that birds can continue to use it as a place to rest.

The area around the monastery was fenced off, having been renovated by the Mongolian government in 2016. The gate was flanked by two buildings: a park ranger station on one side and the central office for a tourist camp on the other. The presence of these stations highlighted the multiplicity of ways that heritage is consumed at places like Süm Khökh Bürd. The ranger station indicates the wetland surrounding the ruins as a protected natural zone. Meanwhile, the tourist camp, with yurts for rent set up within the fenced-off area, uses the ruins' status as an artifact of Mongolia's tangible cultural heritage as a source of value for the domestic tourism industry.

Both buildings were empty and the gate hung open, so we let ourselves in. We followed a stone path that winds around the marsh to the ruins. At the end of the path, a complex of crumbled rooms faced a stage, purportedly first constructed by the Buddhist luminary Dulduityn Danzanravjaa for performances of his plays. Just past the stage, there was new structure, a museum dedicated to the history of the monastery. Like the ranger station and tourist camp, this museum was empty. Looking through the windows, we noticed that it had not yet been filled with exhibits.

There was very little of the monastery itself left standing. What was once a cohesive structure was now a maze of freestanding walls and piles of stone. The roofs of the structure had all fallen in. Even the walls that were still standing sported massive holes. Bayar seemed disconcerted. Gazing through one of these holes, he remarked that the walls looked like they had been blown apart by dynamite.

Kestrels soared about the ruins, using those holes as resting spots. They treated the crumbling, pitted walls as kestrels in other parts of the Gobi treat natural cliffs. I stood on the stage, rebuilt as part of the Mongolian government's 2016 rehabilitation effort, and tried to imagine what it would have been like to perform here when the monastery was still active. Behind me I heard Bayar say, "This is a place of tragedy." When I turned to ask him what he meant, he pointed out an *ovoo* that had been constructed bearing fresh silk sash offerings deep in a collapsed room.

The ruins are populated by a handful of small *ovoo* like this one. Several more dot the ridge line. Just outside the front gate there is a large *ovoo* in the state-constructed style with wooden supports and an even, geometric shape presumably built-up when the site was rehabilitated as an ecologically protected area.

Bayar explained that *ovoo* pop up around abandoned or ruined monasteries "like mushrooms after the rains." Quietly, he added that some people build them and worship at them to assuage the spirits of monks who were killed during the Stalinist purge during the late 1930s. Even though this monastery was ancient and appeared to have fallen out of use before the socialist era, it bore markers of that period's state violence.

As we retraced our steps back out of the ruins, Bayar asked if I believed in ghosts. Nodding back over the water to the amphitheater, he continued. "People say the ghosts of monks get trapped in these monasteries. Some people even come out to places like this at night looking for lights." As we departed, a group of people, well dressed in the traditional style, had found a way into the ruins through the back and were carefully adorning its *ovoo* with ritual sashes. Bayar insisted that we pay our respects to that large, seemingly state-constructed *ovoo* before we leave, to help maintain the wetland's ecosystem.

In the previous chapter, Chuluun and Tsegii were not confident in the rejuvenation of the *takhi* population. They addressed this concern with a cultural heritage practice, long-song, to support the *takhi*'s rehabilitation. Here, the wetland rehabilitation surrounding this demolished monastery did not include a conciliation of the spirits at the site. So, people snuck in to construct small *ovoo* around the site to incorporate a cultural heritage practice into the rehabilitation.

At this monastery, natural heritage, cultural heritage, and the "negative heritage" (Meskell 2002) of commemorated violence intersect. The heritage of this site operates on a nonlinear moral temporality. The *ovoo* here stand as bulwarks against a future which promises desertification and climate change on behalf of a wetland and the birds who rely on it. The very same *ovoo* work as reminders of the violence of Soviet pseudo-colonialism and Stalinist purges and as offerings to the spirits of the dead at a monastery that likely fell to ruin long before the socialist period began. The *ovoo* are witnesses to the ghosts of monks who are said to haunt the monastery and play out the deaths of other monks who would be killed centuries after they had passed away, on a stage for an audience of ghost-hunting humans and migrating birds.

Conclusion

To return to the legend at the start of this chapter, it is notable that mountain spirits and people in the story occupy the same environment but are unable to understand each other without the intervention of *ovoo*. Their worlds overlap just enough to create discord. In each of the above examples, *ovoo* act as mediators, transmitting the wills and needs of nonhuman animals, mountains, and ghosts with humans. The designation of *ovoo*-related worship practices as heritage implicates them and the networks they mediate for in broader structures of transnational consumption. To frame heritage as either a quest for state hegemony or a form of political subversion for oppressed groups misses the nonhuman actors engaging with, constituting, and shaping heritage sites and practices.

Bayar, Zulaa, and Tüvshee engaged in what they described as mutual preservation with *ovoo* and the multispecies networks that those *ovoo* represent. In their own ways they each tied their spiritual, financial, and physical health to the health of these *ovoo*. They have all been faced with difficult situations arising from transnational structures, and they work through *ovoo* to find solutions that mobilize a more-than-human web of social relations.

However, in resolving their first conflict they are invariably led to a second. Bayar's solution to the environmental and spiritual degradation that come with tourism puts him into conflict with local people and animals in the areas he tries to restore. Tüvshee and Zulaa's solution to concerns of health and financial stability is subject to the ire of Western consumers, who use the inscription of spiritual practices and spaces as internationally valuable heritage to stake claims on the musicians' right to mobilize their own cultural resources. As the first pass around the *ovoo* is never enough to complete a ritual, these three continue to work through *ovoo* to find further solutions to these conflicts. With each pass, another stone is added, creating artifacts that grow and spread in number in commemoration of these struggles.

CHAPTER 6

THE SUN OVER THE PLACID WORLD RISES AGAIN

At the end of the summer in 2018 I spoke with Tuyaa, the musicologist, in her office in the National Conservatory. During this interview I asked her what the future holds for pastoral musical practices, such as songs that evoke horse gaits or that calm livestock during nursing. She told me, in an even, matter-of-fact tone, "We are not there yet. In twenty years, when the countryside is gone, I do not know what will happen. For now, we still have nature, so we have not become disconnected. Even if the countryside is destroyed, I do not think we will disconnect from nature." She continued, "It is the shape of our hearts, the key Mongolian people are tuned to."

A quiet moment passed between us. "Our world ended once before, you know," Tuyaa added. "In 1937." She was referring to the Great Purge, an offshoot of Stalinist purges that took place in Mongolia from 1937 to 1939 supported by the Red Army of the Soviet Union. The purge targeted ethnic minorities (particularly Buryat and Kazakh people), Buddhist lamas, and the intelligentsia, leading to the deaths of up to thirty-five thousand people, or 5 percent of the population of the country (Bawden 1989, 328–31; Atwood 2004, 209–10; Kuromiya 2014, 787).[*]

---

[*] I side with Bawden in his interpretation that though the purges were nominally overseen by Choibalsan, the leader of the Mongolian People's Republic, the Great Purge can be seen primarily as an act of violence perpetrated by the USSR (1989, 329).

Tuyaa continued, "During the transition to socialism, much was lost. Records were destroyed, artists thrown in jail or killed. In the 1940s, '50s, and '60s we wanted to replenish our culture. We listened to our elders, to livestock and the land and we revitalized." Shortly after giving this reassurance, she added, "Maybe the world will end, but even if the earth is destroyed, we have sent a recording of 'Uyakhan Zambuu Tiviin Naran' ('The Sun over the Placid World') into outer space on a satellite, so that whoever comes after will know that there were wise, beautiful souls who lived here." She staked this claim not as a joke, nor necessarily as a statement of genuine belief. Rather, this was poetic speculation on her part—true in meaning whether or not these events are literally meant to come to pass.

Though this kind of direct reference to socialist-era repression was somewhat rare in my interviews, similar images of this cycle of destruction and regeneration emerged repeatedly. This cycle came through in an interview at the University of Arts and Culture with Baatar, a horse fiddle teacher specializing in long-song who himself pursued dual training as a classical musician at the National Conservatory and as a traditional musician by seeking tutelage in rural southeastern Mongolia. He told me that he is not worried about his mostly urban students' abilities to learn what he considers to be nomadic music saying, "We have forgotten so much, but the fiddle remembers. More importantly, the fiddle reminds us."

Manduhai Buyandelger (2013) argues that during and after the socialist period, the Mongolian state set about to suppress the stories of the victims of oppression and supplant them with new, officially sanctioned narratives through what she calls "technologies of forgetting" (67). As she describes, recovery from the violent history of the purges, for both humans and spirits, required acts of remembering (84). For Baatar, it is not only humans who can "remember" in ways that disrupt the violent history of colonial oppression. The music and its instrument carry more-than-human counter-histories that people can draw upon for revitalizing ways of being that have been twice suppressed, first under socialism and again under capitalism.

Perhaps Tuyaa's apocalyptic, more-than-terrestrial thinking is a useful heuristic for approaching the Anthropocene in postsocialist societies. For Tuyaa, late capitalism and the global ecological disasters it promises are framed as another installment of a cycle of world-ending events tied to global, colonial modernist movements. The end of the world looms ominously in the forefront of her mind, informed by personal, familial, and cultural memories of a world that ended recently.

It is striking that Tuyaa foregrounds the role of animals and rural landscapes in the rebuilding process. She describes these nonhumans as equals to knowledgeable elders, as beings with perspectives that are vital to surviving world-ending violences. Baatar brings the horse fiddle itself into this network of actors in his quote above. Nonhumans stood as allies for recovering from the last time Tuyaa's world ended and remain so in the blueprint she laid out for recovering again.

Mongolia is a country on the precipice. Climate change is already having devastating effects on the environment in the country. Community resilience in the face of those effects is hamstrung by neoliberal policies that limit social services available to rural people whose subsistence livelihoods are directly under threat (Janes and Chuluundorj 2015). Capitalism, though only thirty years old in Mongolia, is falling apart all over the world and leaving pockets of ruin in which people have started building new futures in multispecies collaboration (Tsing 2015).

Furthermore, other potential nonhumans, those entities that might come after humans have destroyed this earth, stand in Tuyaa's projection as critical consumers of Mongolian cultural heritage. Recordings of music sent off-planet present Tuyaa an opportunity to present a counter argument to future witnesses of Earth's destruction, to assert the existence of people like her who love and live with nature, but who have little power to slow down its destruction. Tuyaa made this statement with the ontological agnosticism of an ethnographer. This, too, is a kind of survival.

In this chapter, I pick up on the science fiction element in Tuyaa's assertion to look for ways that Mongolian musicians have played with the speculative. Faced with the end of the socialist world and the potential upcoming end of the capitalist world, popular and folk musicians alike turn to speculation to imagine other futures. I first highlight the ways that rock and folk-rock performers work the speculative into their compositions. Then I follow the story of "Uyakhan Zambuu Tiviin Naran" as singers pass the song down through the end of two worlds.

The Speculative and the Shamanic Slot

Tuyaa uses speculative imagining to anticipate worlds to come after climate change and colonialism have rendered the current one uninhabitable. Imagining new futures in this way and entrusting her heritage to them is a form of Indigenous resilience. In Mongolia, music is a particularly fruitful arena for speculative imagining.

Speculative fiction and speculation in nonfiction, particularly ethnography, are inextricably tied to the European imperial project. For Said (1994), European imperialism would not be possible without the emergence of the novel as a literary form. Trouillot (2003) similarly contends that through both fiction and nonfiction, Western writers and anthropologists have created the ideological core imperialism by rhetorically constructing the Elsewheres against which the West could be defined (22–23). Speculation runs through both the novel and the ethnography as a way to imagine societies, their pasts and futures, into ordered relation.

Science fiction has been a vehicle through which European colonialists have developed, reflected on, and refined the colonial gaze since the nineteenth century (Rieder 2008). This genre has been a way for colonizers to explore imperial desires and fears by mobilizing ideas about native people and create new natives in imaginary places. Despite, or more accurately because of, the colonizing history of speculative fiction, Indigenous people living in colonial and postcolonial conditions play with those tropes. Through their own approaches to speculative fiction and ethnography, native artists break those colonial genres down to refract a variety of possible futures. In Mongolia, performers bring this inversion into music, using the language of science fiction to transform cultural heritage into a resource for future-building.

At the onset of the Soviet Union, visitors from outer space figured strongly in white imaginations of Mongolia, Central Asia, and Indigenous Siberia. Inspired by the mysterious 1908 explosion in central Siberia known as the Tunguska Event, a subgenre of science fiction cropped up in Russia in the 1920s that framed the Asian inhabitants of the Soviet project as otherworldly themselves. This body of literature portrayed Indigenous Siberians as people who were so "uncivilized" that their traditional bodies of knowledge would be potentially necessary for understanding alien life forms (Bruno 2022).

The USSR's incorporation of Siberia was built on the Russian Tsardom's preexisting colonization of the region, going as far back as the seventeenth century (Kivelson 2006). Following the Orientalist model (Said 1979), Moscow sought to build and legitimize its empire by making itself into The West and rendering the Central Asian steppe and Siberia as The Orient. The Soviet project built on top of those imperial ambitions, using ethnographic constructions of Central Asian and Siberia societies to justify their colonization and assumption into the USSR (Hirsch 2005).

Fiction played a role in this project as well. The intergalactic Orientalism of Tunguska Event literature further dehumanized Indigenous Siberian people and tied them to distant planets as a form of discursive disentanglement of native people from the region. Framing Indigenous people as otherworldly is a way to delegitimize their claims to land, a corollary to the Soviet Union's naturalization of colonial claims to land through mechanisms of "settling" (Thompson 2008).

The Soviet Union actualized these colonial imaginaries by centering their push toward technologies of the future in the Asian steppe and taiga. Starting in 1957, the USSR based its space program out of Baikonur in the Kazakh SSR, where the longest-running and largest space complex on the planet stays in operation to this day as the (Kopack 2019, 556). In 1961, when cosmonaut Yuri Gagarin became the first human being in outer space, he launched off from the Kazakh steppe (Kassenova 2022, 130). At the same time, on the other side of the Kazakh SSR, the Soviet Union based their experimentations with nuclear energy and weaponry in Semipalatinsk (Kassenova 2022). These projects were political realizations of the imaginaries first established by the Orientalizing science fiction mentioned earlier. In other words, these projects are examples of an imperial power making its future imaginaries real by placing their progress into space and the nuclear age in sacrifice zones in Indigenous territories.

Creating sacrifice zones on Native land is not unique to the Soviet Union; it is a core settler colonial project worldwide. On the other side of the Cold War, the United States was undertaking this project at the same time. The United States also used speculation to primordialize and deterritorialize Indigenous people, first through ethnography (Znamenski 2007), then through science fiction (Grewell 2001). Like the USSR, the United States centered their nuclear future on Native territory, using the deterritorializing logic of this speculative thinking to justify transforming Navajo territory into a sacrifice zone (Voyles 2015).

In both cases, colonial speculation rendered Indigenous people as symbols of humanity's deep past, but also as representatives of humanity's potential future. Native people are represented as prehistoric people brought through time to be the stewards of the homelands of the space race and nuclear technology. The overlap between Soviet and United States imaginaries of native people is exemplified through the term "shaman."

In both scholarship and popular media in the West, spiritual practitioners from a wide variety of traditions throughout the New World have been labeled with the title "shaman," a Siberian word referring to a very specific body of practice. Even my usage of "shamanism" instead of the more accurate term *böö mörgöl* to refer to Buryat and Mongolian traditional practices is a concession to the ubiquity of this term to refer to ecstatic religious practices. This rhetorical elision of cultural differences within and across Siberia and the Amazon, two massive regions home to many peoples and histories on opposite sides of the planet, places them within what I call the "shamanic slot."

The term "shaman" most likely comes to use from Tungusic languages (such as Evenki or Manchu) and describes a person from those communities who enters a state of trance through the use of music to channel spirits of ancestors or other supernatural entities (Znamenski 2007). Contemporary scholarship on religious life throughout nomadic Northeast Asia typically uses the term "shamanism" as a calque for a variety of local practices based on the proximity of the communities of practice and similarities in the meaning and performance of certain rituals. For example, Willerslev (2007) uses the term to refer to the spiritual practices of Yukaghir hunters, which center the channeling of spirits and draw on similar canons of knowledge as other forms of Siberian shamanism. Likewise, Hamayon (1990) and Buyandelger (2013) use the term "shamanism" to refer to Buryat and Mongolian practices which, like Evenki and Yukaghir shamans, use the music of the frame drum and jaw harp to enter the trance state required to channel spirits.

However, ethnographies abound that refer to practitioners of disparate ritual traditions in the Americas, all of whom have different local names with specific meanings, as "shamans" as well (Castaneda 1968; Castro and Skafish 2014; Giraldo Herrera 2018). The term has also entered Anglophone popular culture, as burned-out people in the tech and finance industries in the United States take tours of their own psyches by taking ayahuasca under the guidance of *vegetalistas* from Central or South America, who are renamed "shamans" in English as part of a broader corporatization of Indigenous lifeways (Levy 2016).

In *The Beauty of the Primitive*, Znamenski (2007) traces the extension of the term "shaman" to include Native American practices in the Western imagination to the emergence of a German Romanticist movement in the late eighteenth and early nineteenth centuries that fixated on Indigenous people in Siberia and the Southwestern United States. This Romanticist movement would turn into a twentieth century anti-modern movement, with the groundwork laid in place for "shaman" to be a term for an erstwhile pan-Indigenous spiritual guide for Western people in search of an out from modernity (Znamenski 2007, 364). The popular and academic use of "shaman" in the West to refer to practitioners of Indigenous religions in the Americas today can largely be traced to some key comparative religion scholars in that mid-twentieth century anti-modernist wave, spearheaded by writers such as Mircea Eliade and Carlos Castaneda.

Eliade (1964) was one of the most prominent figures in redefining shamanism as a global religion shared among Indigenous people around the world, based on the shared practice of "ecstasy," otherwise known as the use of a trance or trance-like state as part of religious practice, extending the concept beyond the confines of Siberia. Castaneda (1968) followed up on this definition, centering the concept of shamanism in the Native Mexican Yaqui community and thereby cementing shamanism as a term applied to Native American practices. Critics of Eliade have argued that his work inappropriately and unscientifically lumps together ideas from Native practitioners of widely disparate traditions to create a kind of primitivism that casts Indigenous people in the Americas and Siberia alike as noble savages who carry Paleolithic or primordial religious practices into the contemporary era (Kehoe 1996). The primordialist theorizations of Eliade and his contemporaries would lead to a wave of writing on a category of "shamanism" that freely brings together decontextualized ideas and practices from across Indigenous epistemologies in North Asia, especially Siberia, and the Americas, particularly the Amazon, to the exclusion of ecstatic practices found in other parts of the world (see Harner 1990; Vitebsky 1995).

The shamanic slot enfolds all Indigenous people who have been simultaneously marginalized within and made central to a settler colonial power's creation of its own future. "Shamans" in the shamanic slot, whether Evenki, Mayan, Yanomami, or Buryat, represent a world from before colonialism, rendered ahistorically primitive within the logic of "settler time" (Rifkin 2017). Yet they also represent the capacity to travel to different realities, even when that is not a self-described facet of the spiritual tradition being described.

The shamanic slot gives settlers a way to imagine a future in which the ills of settler colonialism have been undone without settler colonialism itself being challenged. The imaginary that creates the shamanic slot presents the possibility of a world that is simultaneously precolonial (a "natural" world where the effects of climate change have been reversed) and postcolonial (a "civilized," cosmopolitan world where any kind of knowledge, practice, or experience is only a weekend's workshop away). The shamanic slot is the logical end result of imperialist nostalgia (Rosaldo 1989), where mourning for the worlds that colonialism has destroyed leads to the colonizer's desire to recapture those worlds through the shaman as a guide to other ontologies. So, the shaman is presented as an ecologically noble savage with access to ancient, primordial knowledge that should be made available to all, for a price.* At the same time, the shaman is presented as a postcolonial urbanite whose spiritual lineage may be as dubious as it is contemporaneous.**

Imagining Back

Indigenous people are not passive observers in their own stories. Native people in the Americas and Siberia alike are aware of the narratives constructed about themselves. Throughout this book, I have made the case that Mongolian people use heritage, an international institution which absorbs subsistence lifeways into neoliberalism, to build more-than-human futures in preparation for neoliberalism's collapse. This argument has

---

* As seen in the *New Yorker* (Levy 2016).
** As seen in the *New York Times* (Levin 2009).

hinged on the idea that Mongolian people are aware of their placement in the savage slot (Trouillot 2003) and mobilize their cultural resources in ways that play with that position. People in the shamanic slot likewise subvert the ideologies underpinning it, using the dual categorization of their Indigenous practices as primordial and futuristic to create futures beyond the present era of colonialism. Bayar, the tour guide and spiritualist from chapter 5, told me that he explicitly refers to his practice of *böö mörgöl* in English as "shamanism," not in spite of the term's racial baggage, but specifically to generate solidarity with Native American people and other Indigenous people around the world.

Speculative fiction provides spaces for native people to explore what Grace Dillon calls "Indigenous Futurisms," a multiplicity of potential futures for people who have already experienced the world-ending violence of settler colonialism. When Dery (1994) first coined the term "Afrofuturism" to describe speculative work by African American authors, he saw speculative fiction as a way for people in the Africa diaspora to address the problem of building possible futures despite having their collective pasts erased by colonialism (180). Indigenous Futurisms offer a similar potential for native people who have likewise had their histories disrupted by colonial powers. Writing on film, Lempert (2014) argues that science fiction provides a vehicle through which Indigenous people can simultaneously imagine new futures beyond colonialism while also addressing its ongoing effects on their communities.

With the space race, Moscow's fringes exceeded planet Earth. This geopolitical conceptualization would have significant impact on the lives of the people who lived at its terrestrial fringes: Siberia and Central Asia. On the Asian frontiers of the USSR, the colonized steppe and taiga spread from Kyrgyzstan and Kazakhstan northeast up to the Arctic Circle. Authors and artists from all around the region drew on the shared experience of colonization and placement within the shamanic slot to imagine futures where pan-Indigenous solidarity stands in the face of colonial violence. Mongolia is in a unique position as the country that served simultaneously the eastern border of the Soviet Union's terrestrial spread and as the territory where Central Asia and Siberia meet. As such, the country is central to this region and its history, but also on its outskirts.

Authors from colonized regions of the USSR took what Tunguska science fiction had done, using space exploration as a narrative device through which to envision the Soviet project, and adapted it to reflect on the Indigenous experience of that project. White authors saw the potentials and dangers of incredible technological breakthrough in their imaginations of contact with outer space (Bruno 2022). Asian authors, like Kyrgyz science fiction writer Chingiz Aïtmatov, saw an empire seeking a new extraction zone (Banerjee 2018).

In the science fiction novel *The Day Lasts More than a Hundred Years*, Aïtmatov presents a Soviet science exploration apparatus that had made a group of Kazakh locals into outsiders on their own land (Aïtmatov 1983; Banerjee 2018). While his white contemporaries wrote about space exploration to imagine futures yet to come, Aïtmatov uses space exploration to encapsulate a state of affairs that had already come to pass. Russia had already colonized Kazakhstan and begun driving Kazakh people away from their homelands and from their native language.

To take another example, in *Бөөгийн Домог* (*Legend of the Shaman*), Mongolian author Ayurzana Gün-Aajav (2010) brings together themes from ethnographic fiction, magical realism, and climate fiction to craft a story that repurposes the shamanic slot to create international solidarity. The hero of the novel, a disaffected listicle writer from Ulaanbaatar named Tengis, travels to an island in Lake Baikal to learn from a Buryat shaman. Ayurzana starts with a conventional shamanic slot narrative—a modern man seeks out a shaman to guide him into a parallel world away from the woes of capitalist life. However, he replaces the typical white hero with a Mongolian narrator, who grapples with his position as both an insider and an outsider to the shamanic tradition he is learning. During his time in Baikal, Tengis meets a First Nations ethnographer from Canada named Reggie, who has come to Siberia write a book about the island's religious traditions. Through the character of Reggie, Tengis discovers the potential for pan-Indigenous collaboration and solidarity across the shamanic slot.

Musical Science Fiction in Modern Mongolia

In Mongolia, music has been a field where artists have experimented with the speculative and science fiction quite a bit in the twenty-first century. Musicians use the speculative to comment and reflect on the conditions of postsocialism and the strain of neoliberal shock therapy. The speculative element in contemporary Mongolian music has had a transformative effect on the horse fiddle as well, positioning the instrument as central to the creation of distinctly Mongolian futures.

The foundational grunge band Nisvanis* brought science fiction elements into their music to imagine escapes from the conditions of life in Ulaanbaatar in the late 1990s and early 2000s. Though the band started in 1996, their 2006 album *Nisdeg Tavag* (*Flying Saucer*) launched them into a central, lasting position within the Mongolian popular music scene, celebrated with a rooftop concert overlooking Ulaanbaatar. The cover of the album features four grey aliens representing the band members. They sit miserably in the kind of gazebo commonly found in the center of Mongolian apartment complexes as a flying saucer soars over lines of drying laundry. This humorous approach to defamiliarizing life in the country's capital carries throughout the album. Interspersed with tracks about romantic disappointment and urban malaise are songs that narrate the perspectives of aliens and humans alike who desire nothing more than to leave Earth and soar into the stars. A key example is the title track, "Nisdeg Tavag" (table 4).

In this song, Nisvanis highlights how severe the changes to Mongolian society have been in the wake of neoliberal shock therapy by taking the position of an alien who so thoroughly does not recognize the country that he no longer feels like this is his planet. Using this framework, frontman Enkh-Amgalan unspools the subtle but devastating effects of multiple overlapping layers of world-ending colonial violences: corruption, loneliness, poverty, the need for money itself in a system that makes earning it nearly impossible for the majority of people. Even the potential for escape has been contained within the cruel mechanisms of capitalism—the flying saucer has been pawned.

Nisvanis helped develop the sound of Mongolian rock music in the twenty-first century through their humorous but careful use of science fiction contextualized with local aesthetic elements drawn from Buddhism.

---

* The name Nisvanis itself is a playful reclamation of Buddhist concepts appropriated by Western artists. Nisvanis is the Mongolian term for the *kleshas*, the four states of repulsion, egoism, attachment, and fear of death that cloud the mind and cause suffering in Buddhist philosophy. In other words, Nisvanis is the opposite of Nirvana, the choice of name a purposeful inversion of the foundational Seattle grunge band.

TABLE 4 Lyrics for "Nisdeg Tavag" ("Flying Saucer") by Nisvanis (2006)

1.	1.
Танай гариг, танай гариг намайг бачууруулж байна.	Your planet, your planet makes me uneasy.
Таньж мэдэх, таньж мэдэх, таньж мэдэх юу ч алга.	I don't recognize, I don't recognize, I don't recognize any of this.
Тэгээд дээр нь, тэгээд дээр нь, тэгээд дээр нь луйварчид.	And on top of that, on top of that, on top of that, all the schemers.
Тиймээс би, тиймээс би, тиймээс би буцмаар байна.	So I, so I, so I want to go back.
Chorus.	Chorus.
Ломбарднаас нисдэг тавгаа, нисдэг тавгаа авмаар байна.	I want to buy myself a flying saucer, a flying saucer from a pawn shop.
Тэгээд эндээс эндээс би буцмаар байна.	Then I want to go back, away from here, away from here.
Ломбарднаас нисдэг тавгаа, нисдэг тавгаа авмаар байна.	I want to buy myself a flying saucer, a flying saucer from a pawn shop.
Тэгээд эндээс эндээс би буцмаар байна	Then I want to go back, away from here, away from here.
2.	2.
Одоо надад, одоо надад, одоо надад мөнгө ч алга.	Now I, now I, now I don't have any money.
Ойлгож мэдэх, ойлгож мэдэх, ойлгож мэдэх хүн ч алга.	There is no one here who understands, who understands, who understands.
Тэгээд дээр нь, тэгээд дээр нь, тэгээд дээр нь ганцаардаж байна.	And on top of that, on top of that, on top of that, I'm lonely.
Тиймээс би, тиймээс би, тиймээс би буцмаар байна.	So I, so I, so I want to go back.
3.	3.
Шар айраган далай дээр шарсан галуу хөвж явдаг,	Where roast ducks float on an ocean of beer,
Шаналж мөнгө төгрөг хайх хэрэг байдаггүй,	Where you never have to strive for money,
Сургууль гэж байхгүй эрүүлжүүлэх ч байхгүй,	Where school is always out and you never sober up,
Манай гариг эндээс маш хол байдаг юм.	My planet is far away from here.

Throughout the first decade of the twenty-first century, interest in indie rock and grunge music dovetailed with a resurging interest in traditional music in the region. This led to the emergence of folk-rock in Mongolia, and folk-metal in Inner Mongolia, as musicians started to attach electric pick-ups to their horse fiddles and perform polyphonic throat singing alongside the heavy reverb of electric guitars.

The genre of Mongolian folk-rock was typified early on by Altan Urag, the band that popularized the electric horse fiddle. Altan Urag was one of the earliest Mongolian bands to make a major impact in the United States, first through the soundtrack they composed for the 2007 Sergei Bodrov film *Mongol: The Rise of Genghis Khan* and then through their soundtracks for the Netflix series *Marco Polo* in 2014, directed by John Fusco. Altan Urag's sound is dark and ominous. They combine phrasing, rhythm, and acoustic technology from hard rock with traditional, microtonal instruments like the horse fiddle and the *ever büree*, a spiral-shaped horn with a sound similar to a clarinet. The science fiction elements of their music are imprinted directly on the bodies of the fiddle themselves. Rather than the usual horse head carved into the scroll, Altan Urag's electric fiddles are topped with xenomorph heads from the *Alien* film franchise. The xenomorph head is supported by a single crow's talon, perched on top of a skull in the style of Tibetan Buddhist religious art.

The alien-headed fiddles call back to Bilgüün's claim from chapter 1 that the body of the instrument itself is an important part of its meaning and social power. Through the bodies of their fiddles, Altan Urag picked up on speculative elements already present in Mongolian heritage from Buddhist cosmology and bound them aesthetically with monsters of science fiction. These instruments demonstrate a way of thinking about the cultural heritage of the horse fiddle as something that has the capacity to create new futures rather than as simple relics of the past. By siding with the aliens, rather than the American marines who stand as the heroes of the films they are referencing, the performers signal that the future they imagine is counter to the imperial futures that Western speculative fiction creates.

U.S. Americans are often surprised when shown pictures of Ulaanbaatar, where metal sculptures of the titular Predator from the *Predator* film series lurk outside of banks and ride motorcycles made from xenomorph parts (figure 7). *Alien vs. Predator* (Anderson 2004), with its invocation of extraterrestrial activity to explain away the presence of pyramids in South America, is a core text in the construction of the shamanic slot I described above. Though it is not tied to Northern Asia, Mongolian people see affinities with Indigenous people throughout this slot and transform these science fiction aesthetics to their own needs.

FIGURE 7 Statue of the Predator from the *Predator* film series riding a motorcycle made of xenomorph parts from the *Aliens* film series in Ulaanbaatar, Mongolia. Photograph by K. G. Hutchins.

After Altan Urag, elements of the speculative began to spread throughout a variety of genres in the Mongolian popular music scene. Take, for example, rapper Big Gee's song with the folk-rock ensemble Jonon and singer Bayaraa, "Minii Nutgiig Nadad Üldee" ("Leave Me My Homeland"), which pairs lyrics about desertification with a music video depicting wanderers in a postapocalyptic wasteland (Gee and Bayaraa 2011; Irvine 2018). However, it is important to note how central the horse fiddle has been to this speculative wave in popular music.

The Mongolian folk-rock genre recently hit a moment of global popularity through the emergence of the band The HU, through the music videos for their songs "Wolf Totem" and "Yuve Yuve Yu" ("How Strange"), which went internally viral online in 2018 ahead of their first album release the following year (The HU 2019). The HU followed in Altan Urag's footsteps by using electric versions of traditional instruments and outfitting them with unique heads that evoke the aesthetic and political thrust of the band's compositions. The HU's fiddles and electric *tovshuur* lute are carved to resemble heavy-metal versions of horses from metalwork associated with the third century BCE nomadic Xiongnu empire. Through these instruments the band borrows aesthetics from Altan Urag's science fiction and horror-inspired alien heads and combining them with an appeal to a "deep past" (Humphrey 1992) that connects Mongolian heritage with the other nomadic communities of the Altai, Central Asia, and Siberia. In the song that cemented them as an international fixture, "Yuve Yuve Yu," The HU brings the speculative and deep past elements of their music to bear to comment on environmental degradation and on the risks of ethno-nationalist thinking—two of the biggest exports from the Western world to its postcolonies.

What is important for us here is the way that musicians have used this speculative approach to pick up on other ways of imagining futures that were already present in Mongolian heritage. The above examples present an overview of some of the possibilities of the speculative approach in musical heritage. For a more in depth look at how musicians transform musical heritage into speculative future, let us return to Tuyaa's story about sending "The Sun Over the Placid World" into outer space.

Sunset/Sunrise

The tale of "Uyakhan Zambuu Tiviin Naran" is the story of one world ending, a new one beginning, and coming to its own end. The lyrics of the song itself, as discussed in chapter 4, compare the sun's trajectory over the horizon to the span of a person's life. The song carries with it a second story, the history of how singers were able to preserve a song with such heavy Buddhist messaging through the twentieth century, when open religious practice was banned.

"Uyakhan Zambuu Tiviin Naran" is the song most closely associated with Dundgovi province, popularized internationally by professional vocalist Namjilyn Norovbanzad in a series of concerts during the 1970s and '80s. Throughout the Gobi, long-song are vital for ceremonially opening and closing *nair*, those traditional feasts held as part of wedding celebrations and housewarming parties, like the one in this book's introduction. Long-song are so important, and so difficult to master, that a good singer can earn a decent amount of money and pastoral goods during the fall months traveling the countryside as an itinerant long-song singer.

Working as an itinerant singer for *nair* is how Dad'süren made ends meet for the early part of his life, shortly after the purges in the mid-twentieth century. His parents divorced when he was quite young, so he split his formative years with his mother and father. His mother taught him to sing and how to carry out the ritual of the *nair*, and he would travel the countryside with his father, singing at *nair* for food and money to help his parents make ends meet.

In Dundgovi there was a particular monk who had a large canon of long-song committed to memory. His knowledge was especially valuable because he knew *aizam* long-song, extended songs with dozens of stanzas vital to the proper performance of *nair*. These songs are difficult to learn and vocally demanding, with up to sixty-four verses per song and sweeping melodies that surge into falsetto and double falsetto. For one song, he was particularly well known: "Uyakhan Zambuu Tiviin Naran."

"Uyakhan Zambuu Tiviin Naran" is commonly translated as "the Sun over the Placid World" or "Endless Sunshine." Neither translation captures the fact that the song refers not to *delkhii*, the secular term for Earth, but rather to *Zambuu tiv* or Jambudvīpa, the land where humans seek enlightenment in Buddhist cosmology. The openly Buddhist didactic nature of the song made it subject to purge-era repression of religious materials.

In Dad'süren's words:

> I begged the monk to teach me this song, but he refused and refused. He had taught the song to only two people before, two of his novices at the monastery. Both were killed during the purges, so the lama said he would not teach the song anymore for fear that he would invite retributions from the state on any more students. But I bothered him and bothered him about it until he gave in and agreed to teach me on one condition—that I never sing the song for people, that my only audience be the sheep in the fields.

The monk, who had witnessed the destruction of his monastery and the killings of his students, had resigned himself to the idea that his world, the *Zambuu tiv*, would not survive him. Socialist modernity was coming to destroy and replace the Buddhist world, so he swore Dad'süren to keep his knowledge of this song, and the world it contained, a secret. Through this song, he ferried wisdom from the old world into the new one.

For many years Dad'süren kept his promise to keep the song secret. He continued to sing the song while tending to his livestock, only when he knew there were no other humans around to hear him. As he recalled this period of his life, he made it clear that the sheep were listening, and he sang to keep them calm. In chapter 3, Dad'süren asserted that the sheep in the fields were his only audience for many years. The song he sang them was "Uyakhan Zambuu Tiviin Naran."

In subsequent interviews, Dad'süren and Buyaa both insisted that their livestock were indeed listening and responding to their songs. They pointed to two types of evidence to back this claim. Like the other herders described in the third chapter, they paid close attention to the animals' affective responses to their singing, like increased milk production. They also paid attention to social responses, like the repaired relationships between estranged mothers and youths. In Dad'süren's story, he described sheep as shared bearers of "Uyakhan Zambuu Tiviin Naran," the burden of this song held up by a human singer and a nonhuman audience.

This song demonstrates a way of surviving a kind of apocalypse through musical collaboration with nonhuman animals. By taking sheep as critical audiences for his singing, Dad'süren kept an oral religious text alive through a period when religious texts were outlawed and its previous knowledge-bearers had been killed by the state. He carried knowledge from the old Gobi over into the new Gobi.

◍

Years later, another long-song singer from Dundgovi named Norovbanzad heard that Dad'süren knew this song and came to request he teach her. He told her the same story that his teacher told him, arguing that it was not a safe song to teach. Norovbanzad reassured him "the purges are over, people are starting to practice religion again, you needn't worry." Just as Dad'süren had kept at the monk, Norovbanzad kept at Dad'süren until he agreed finally to teach her the song.

Norovbanzad would soon become one of the most famous and beloved singers in Mongolia. In 1978, she went international, recording a version of "Uyakhan Zambuu Tiviin Naran" for the transnational project *Musical Voices of Asia*. This performance would earn her, and the once nearly lost long-song, a wide audience beyond the Iron Curtain.

When Dad'süren heard Norovbanzad's version of the song on the radio, he was troubled. He called her and asked, "Did I teach you wrong or did you learn wrong?" The version she performed was different, with lyrics that lacked many of the Buddhist references that originally made "Uyakhan Zambuu Tiviin Naran" a subversive piece of music. She told him, "No, no you taught me well, and I learned well, but before I could record, some representatives from the party sat with me and worked through what I could and could not sing on the radio." Though the performance of the song was no longer banned outright, it was still subject to close editing by government representatives, one of the Mongolian state's "technologies of forgetting" during the socialist period (Buyandelger 2013).

Into the twenty-first century, Norovbanzad's recording of this song is still well-loved in postsocialist Mongolia. Several of my interlocutors joked that they should have made it the national anthem of the newly democratic Mongolia back in 1991. In a way, this song does represent the current era in the country well, as elements of traditional knowledge maintained through the transmission of cultural heritage are important assets to Mongolian people who are now revitalizing spiritual practices that were repressed during the twentieth century. These practices, like the edited lyrics of Norovbanzad's recording, bear the marks of socialist-era repression nonetheless.

In addition to representing Mongolia to the world, Norovbanzad's recording of the song is what Tuyaa said will represent the world to whoever comes after humanity. In 2017, Mongolia launched its first ever satellite into space as part of the multinational BIRDS project. The Kyushu Institute of Technology supported a team of students from Mongolia, Ghana, Nigeria, and Bangladesh to send CubeSats representing each of their countries into orbit on SpaceX's Falcon 9 rocket. The engineering students uploaded music in the form of MIDI files to these small, cube-shaped satellites, which then transmitted the songs as radio waves. If you have a HAM radio, you can even tune in. Though the only song officially uploaded to Mongolia's CubeSat is the national anthem, like all good radio stations, they take requests.

Having interviewed Dad'süren herself, Tuyaa knew his story and many others like it. She took to heart the lesson that a people can make a future for their world by entrusting it to a more-than-human audience. Facing a future without habitable pastures for humans or sheep, she had to look farther afield, hoping that "Uyakhan Zambuu Tiviin Naran" being beamed onto a satellite will find an audience from another world.

Once again, this song, and the memories of the men, women, and sheep entangled with it, have been put in the hands of a nonhuman. Just as Dad'süren once sang the song to sheep as a way of maintaining a history at the edge of extermination, Norovbanzad's voice carried the song into the cosmos, and with it a heritage of Earth as it teeters on the edge of destruction. Not any heritage, but a Gobi heritage, where the environment and the people who dwell within it are among the first to experience this destruction. Heritage is a form of a past-making, but it can be used as a form of future-making too. As Dad'süren and Tuyaa demonstrate, for heritage to be future-making, it must be a more-than-human endeavor.

EPILOGUE

Eternity in the Desert

Traveling back to Ulaanbaatar from Süm Khökh Burd, the hunting and tour guide Bayar and I unexpectedly happened upon an active monastery. On top of a hill covered in volcanic rock sat a jet-black, four-story temple with gold detail work on the eaves depicting snarling yellow dragons. Arrayed out in a semi-circle in front of the monastery were a couple of small buildings alongside nomadic felt tents of different sizes.

At first the only living being in sight was a fat, orange temple cat, sunning itself in front of one of the gold-painted buildings. As we approached, Bayar pointed out that this building must be a shrine to Manjushri, the bodhisattva associated with insight. There we were greeted gruffly by a young monk with a Khangai mountain accent. He told us the monastery is named Choir.* This, the monk told us, was the main monastery serving the region.

The monk declined to give his name, though he did agree to a short interview with me and Bayar. He led us to the main building, guiding us past the volcanic stone outcroppings that jutted out from the steps up to the black tower. Facing that main building sat a pinkish concrete statue of

---

* From Tibetan *chos grwa*, meaning a school for Buddhist instruction, a not-uncommon name for a temple in Mongolia.

the national hero Damdin Sükhbaatar on horseback, strikingly similar to the equestrian statue in the middle of Ulaanbaatar's central square.

In fact, according to the monk, it was the equestrian hero statue from Ulaanbaatar during the socialist era. In 2011, when the government built a taller version out of sturdier materials, a wealthy Dundgovi donor brought the old statue to Choir. On hearing that, Bayar excitedly exclaimed, "This is my childhood here," and snapped a picture on his phone. Sükhbaatar and the monastery sat together in the desert, staring at each other for the foreseeable future.

The monastery was as impressive inside as out. The eastern and western walls were lined with large aquariums full of koi fish. Two rows of heavy wooden seats with intricate carvings of swallows and blossoming flowers led to an impressive altar. In the northwestern corner, a spiral of clear plastic stairs wound up to the third floor, while on the northeast side a small replica of a nomadic tent cut from that same clear plastic material guarded the staircase down to the archives. The ceiling was painted with yellow dragons. More gold-painted dragon reliefs adorned four thick columns that were sheathed in thick plastic protective sleeves.

The monk directed our attention to both the sturdiness of the construction and the beauty of the ornamentation. "See the walls," he said, gesturing toward the nearest one. "Built thick, and sturdy. See the columns, that paint is made of gold, and they are protected by the clear plastic outer shell." When I asked him why they bothered protecting the columns with the plastic covers, he replied,

> We did this for two reasons, but they both boil down to one basic idea: we want the place to last. We want it to be well built and maintained enough that people will keep being able to come and use it for generations. We also want it to be beautiful enough that they will recall it fondly. A person who came here as a child should be able to take their grandchildren here and rejoice in its continued beauty.

> The second reason is a bit grander of scale. The goal of our Buddhism is to elevate and educate humankind. Once humans have developed to the point where they are no longer violent—to nature, to each other, and to animals—then and only then Buddha the teacher can depart and his successor, Maitreya, will come to teach humans the great knowledge and

technologies of the universe. We built this temple to last, so that in 2,500 years or however long it takes, elevated people living in the Maitreya era can come see it and know that this was the work of the humans who lived in the Buddha era.

The monk described a future beyond capitalism and environmental degradation. To achieve this future, humanity would have to become nonviolent, to ourselves and nonhumans alike. He described a "gentle world." In other words, the world he described is an *uyakhan Zambuu tiv*, the "placid world" of Buddhist cosmology in which humans engage in peaceful relations with their fellow-beings featured in the long-song "Uyakhan Zambuu Tiviin Naran."

This monastery is a piece of cultural heritage that has been specifically curated to appeal to both current humans and the people of the Maitreya era—ascended beings who are neither human nor entirely nonhuman. The monk's description of how the monastery would show Maitreyans that Buddha-era humans were capable of beauty and insight reminded me of Tuyaa's idea that beaming "Uyakhan Zambuu Tiviin Naran" into outer space would show whoever came after humanity disappeared that there were great artists on Earth. This monk, like Tuyaa, was involved in curating a heritage that would survive beyond, into a postcapitalist future, for the benefit of a group of beings that are themselves beyond humanity. The monk's vision of the future was utopian, while Tuyaa's was dystopian, but survival into both depended on cooperation between humans, nonhumans, and the landscape.

Tuyaa and this monk both imagined the potential for other futures beyond capitalist modernity. Both described rural, Mongolian, semi-desert futures that stretch out far beyond the destruction of the Mongolian landscape, and potentially beyond the destruction, or at least disappearance, of human life on Earth. Throughout this book, I have presented the perspectives of musicians, herders, and heritage bearers as they work toward creating alternatives to modernity from within modern institutions, using modernist bureaucracies. Heritage is the key to building these alternatives because it allows people to forge more-than-human relationships that challenge the nature/culture binary underpinning modernity.

The horse fiddle is emblematic of this approach to heritage. In the first chapter, horse fiddle teachers Ganbold and Tüvshee along with Tuyaa, all working from conservatories in Ulaanbaatar, centered this fiddle in the ways they used heritage to imagine a variety of alternatives to the secular, modernist idea of a disenchanted world. They each offered perspectives on what it means for the horse fiddle, a musical instrument and element of cultural heritage, to have a *süns*, or "spirit." Their viewpoints drew the agency of the instrument into three distinct ontological frames. Despite the differences in how Ganbold, Tüvshee, and Tuyaa describe the power of the fiddle, all three used it to critically examine their relationships with nonhumans from within the confines of modernist institutions.

Throughout chapters 2, 3, and 4, singers and fiddlers used their music to reflect on their relationships with nonhuman animals. Each example highlights a close aesthetic and philosophical connection between music, especially the horse fiddle and long-song, and animals. Camels, cattle, sheep, goats, and horses show up repeatedly as vital collaborators in the transmission of this cultural heritage.

The second chapter engaged the use of heritage at urban music institutions. Multiple horse fiddle teachers based out of the National Conservatory, the University of Arts and Sciences, and the National Philharmonic claimed that nonhuman animals, especially horses, cattle, and camels, are vital resources for learning music. Though the sounds and movements of these animals may be considered important by the teachers, the Western institutional histories of the conservatories that house music education make it difficult to incorporate them into mainstream music education. To integrate the bodily movements of these livestock animals in the transmission of heritage genres, these fiddle teachers had to transform the institutional rhythms of conservatory education.

While the second chapter considered the role of animals in music education, chapter 3 asked what potentials arise when animals are treated as critical audiences for heritage music. In rural Dundgovi, herders Byambaa and Buyaa used traditional song to build relationships between orphaned lambs and new mothers. In these performances, heritage music enabled human herders to engage socially across species boundaries.

Chapter 4 turned to Chuluun and Tsegii, who experimented with performing music for wild animals rather than livestock. They strove to build new relationships with the recently repopulated community of wild *takhi* horses at Hustai National Park through the use of long-song. Through their performances, they identified these horses as bearers of a shared heritage, both natural and cultural. It is significant that in the end, Chuluun and Tsegii disagreed on whether their singing was successful. Their disagreement highlights the ambiguity inherent to new more-than-human relationships that people build in the wake of ecological disasters such as the extinction of *takhi* in central Mongolia during the twentieth century.

Chapters 5 and 6 explored how musical heritage can be entangled in broader networks of relation. In addition to humans and nonhuman animals, the total field of human and nonhuman agents involved in the performance of cultural heritage includes nonliving entities as well. Performers Tüvshee and Zulaa took these geological features as critical audiences for long-song, a role played by horses and sheep in the previous chapters.

The potential for using musical heritage to build more-than-human relationships opens space for imagining futures beyond neoliberalism. These futures can take a variety of forms, as seen in chapter 6. From professional musicians like the members of Altan Urag to herders like Dad'süren, performers use the horse fiddle to imagine futures that pull together Buddhist cosmology, folklore, and science fiction.

Throughout this book, my argument has not been that the political designation of cultural practices as "heritage" is exclusively an emancipatory act that people use to destabilize hegemony of neoliberal modernity. Nor have I argued that the performance of heritage is exclusively a form of future-making. Nationalism and nostalgia run through each of the situations I have discussed. However, I want to highlight the potential for people to use heritage to access alternatives to modernity in which the entanglement of nature and culture is not only recognized, but supported through nondestructive relations between humans, nonhuman animals, and the land.

I have focused primarily on interactions with musicians connected in one way or another to urban, postsocialist institutions. As such, their primary method of engaging with more-than-human futures is through heritage, the institutionalized version of more-than-human cultural practices. As climate change promises increasing ecological devastation throughout Mongolia and across the world, this has been the exploration of just one possible avenue of future-making among many.

Climate change, alienation, and neoliberal exploitation are not conditions unique to Mongolia. People in colonial metropoles are currently learning the hard way that the consequences of capitalism's push for endless growth cannot be contained to a finite number of sacrifice zones. However, Mongolian people have watched their world end before. Building more-than-human networks of relation that are resilient in the face of ecological catastrophes will require us to look to people who have already faced these issues and to consider strategies that are outside of the conventions of Western modernist thinking.

As the Gobi transforms from semi-arid steppe into desert, a direct result of climate change and colonialism, the people who call the Gobi home are faced with the end of a world. The people I worked with used music to build relationships to recover and to imagine futures outside of the totalizing box of capitalist isolation. Dad'süren saw a way forward through his acts of care for his sheep, which had once protected him in the world-ending tumult of his youth. Chuluun saw a similar potential in crafting a kind of multispecies allyship with wild horses, themselves emblematic of a recovery from colonial ecocide by their return from the brink of extinction.

Not everyone saw potentials for surviving the next round of apocalypse to come to the country. However, they did not ignore climate change, nor did they embrace nihilism. In their own ways, the monk of Choir monastery, Tuyaa, and many others imagined further into the future. They dedicated their cultural heritage to whatever intelligent life might one day trawl Earth for relics from the bygone eras of human activity.

The monks of Choir monastery carry out ceremonies for local people every now and again. They read their sutras. They practice nonviolence toward animals by patiently caring for the koi in their massive fish tanks and whatever stray cats wander out of the sagebrush. They do all of this under the watchful gaze of the statue depicting Mongolia's hero of communism, Sükhbaatar. These monks placed their monastery in the red and dusty heart of desertification because, despite their daily acts of devotion, this monastery is not for the present era. They are tending to a piece of living heritage, entrusted to the desert. As the head monk told me, "The desert destroys, it's true. But the desert also preserves."

BIBLIOGRAPHY

Aïtmatov, Chingiz. 1983. *The Day Lasts More than a Hundred Years*. Bloomington: Indiana University Press.

Anderson, E. N. 1996. *Ecologies of the Heart: Emotion, Belief, and the Environment*. New York: Oxford University Press.

Anderson, Paul, dir. 2004. *Alien vs. Predator*. 20th Century Fox.

Asad, Talal. 2003. *Formations of the Secular: Christianity, Islam, Modernity*. Cultural Memory in the Present. Stanford, Calif: Stanford University Press.

Atwood, Christopher Pratt. 2004. *Encyclopedia of Mongolia and the Mongol Empire*. Facts on File Library of World History. New York: Facts On File.

Banerjee, Anindita. 2018. "Atoms, Aliens, and Compound Crises: Central Asia's Nuclear Fantastic." *Science Fiction Studies* 45 (3): 454–68. https://doi.org/10.5621/sciefictstud.45.3.0454.

Bawden, Charles R. 1989. *The Modern History of Mongolia*. 2nd ed. KPI Paperbacks. London: Kegan Paul International.

Bekenov, A. B., Iu. A. Grachev, and E. J. Milner-Gulland. 1998. "The Ecology and Management of the Saiga Antelope in Kazakhstan." *Mammal Review* 28 (1): 1–52. https://doi.org/10.1046/j.1365-2907.1998.281024.x.

Berkes, Fikret, Johan Colding, and Carl Folke. 2000. "Rediscovery of Traditional Ecological Knowledge as Adaptive Management." *Ecological Applications* 10 (5): 1251–62. https://doi.org/10.1890/1051-0761(2000)010[1251:ROTEKA]2.0.CO;2.

Biraa, L. 2017. *Mongol Temeenii Tüükhen Öv, Soyol*. Ulaanbaatar: Edmarket.

Bizas, Eleni. 2014. *Learning Senegalese Sabar: Dancers and Embodiment in New York and Dakar*. Dance and Performance Studies, Vol. 6. New York: Berghahn Books.

Blanchette, Alex. 2020. *Porkopolis: American Animality, Standardized Life, and the Factory Farm.* Durham, N.C.: Duke University Press.

Bloch, Alexia. 2004. *Red Ties and Residential Schools: Indigenous Siberians in a Post-Soviet State.* Philadelphia: University of Pennsylvania Press.

Bodrov, Sergei, dir. 2007. *Mongol: The Rise of Genghis Khan.* Nashe Kino.

Bökönyi, Sándor. 1974. *The Przevalsky Horse.* London: Souvenir Press.

Bortolotto, Chiara. 2007. "From Objects to Processes: UNESCO's 'Intangible Cultural Heritage.'" *Journal of Museum Ethnography,* no. 19, 21–33.

Bouman, Inge, and Jan Bouman. 1994. "The History of Przewalski's Horse." In *Przewalski's Horse: The History and Biology of an Endangered Species,* edited by Lee Boyd and Katherine A. Houpt, 5–38. New York: SUNY Press.

Bruno, Andy. 2022. "Atomic Visitors from Outer Space: The Tunguska Nuclear Hypothesis in Soviet Technological Imagination." *Russian Review* 81 (1): 92–109. https://doi.org/10.1111/russ.12348.

Bubandt, Nils. 2017. "Anthropocene Uncanny: Nonsecular Approaches to Environmental Change." *AURA Working Papers* 3:2–18.

Buchanan, Donna Anne. 2006. *Performing Democracy: Bulgarian Music and Musicians in Transition.* Chicago Studies in Ethnomusicology. Chicago: University of Chicago Press.

Bulag, Uradyn Erden. 1998. *Nationalism and Hybridity in Mongolia.* Oxford Studies in Social and Cultural Anthropology. Oxford: Oxford University Press.

Buyandelger, Manduhai. 2013. *Tragic Spirits: Shamanism, Memory, and Gender in Contemporary Mongolia.* Chicago: University of Chicago Press.

Byrne, David. 2009. "A Critique of Unfeeling Heritage." In *Intangible Heritage,* edited by Laurajane Smith and N. Akagawa, 229–52. New York: Routledge.

Cadena, Marisol de la. 2015. *Earth Beings: Ecologies of Practice across Andean Worlds.* The Lewis Henry Morgan Lectures, 2011. Durham, N.C.: Duke University Press.

Camal, Jerome. 2016. "Putting the Drum in Conundrum: Guadeloupean Gwoka, Intangible Cultural Heritage and Postnationalism." *International Journal of Heritage Studies* 22 (5): 395–410. https://doi.org/10.1080/13527258.2015.1028959.

Campbell, Ake. 1951. "Herdsman's Song and Yoik in Northern Sweden." *Journal of the International Folk Music Council* 3 (March): 64–67. https://doi.org/10.2307/835777.

Casanova, José. 2009. "The Secular and Secularisms." *Social Research* 76 (4): 1049–66.

Castaneda, Carlos. 1968. *The Teachings of Don Juan: A Yaqui Way of Knowledge.* Berkeley: University of California Press.

Castro, Eduardo Batalha Viveiros de, and Peter Skafish. 2014. *Cannibal Metaphysics: For a Post-Structural Anthropology.* Minneapolis, M.N.: Univocal.

Chee, Liz P. Y. 2021. *Mao's Bestiary: Medicinal Animals and Modern China.* Experimental Futures: Technological Lives, Scientific Arts, Anthropological Voices. Durham, N.C.: Duke University Press.

Cleere, Henry. 2001. "The Uneasy Bedfellows: Universality and Cultural Heritage." In *Destruction and Conservation of Cultural Property,* edited by Robert Layton, Peter G. Stone, and Julian Thomas, 22–29. New York: Routledge.

Cui, Dan, Dianting Wu, Jingjing Liu, Ye Xiao, Batchuluun Yembuu, and Zolzaya Adiya. 2019. "Understanding Urbanization and Its Impact on the Livelihood Levels of Urban Residents in Ulaanbaatar, Mongolia." *Growth and Change* 50 (2): 745–74. https://doi.org/10.1111/grow.12285.

Curtis, David. 2006. "Mobilising Rural Communities to Achieve Environmental Sustainability Using the Arts." *Agricultural Economics Review* 7 (1): 1–11.

Dagvadorj, J. 2016. *Büüvein Duu*. Ulaanbaatar: Soyombo Printing.

Daly, Lewis, Katherine French, Theresa L. Miller, and Luíseach Nic Eoin. 2016. "Integrating Ontology into Ethnobotanical Research." *Journal of Ethnobiology* 36 (1): 1–9. https://doi.org/10.2993/0278-0771-36.1.1.

Danzan, Enkhtsetseg. 2007. *Egshigle, Khuur Min': Tele Yariltslaga*. Ulaanbaatar: Erdenezul Press.

Davaa, Byambasuren, and Luigi Falorni, dirs. 2003. *The Story of the Weeping Camel*. ThinkFilm.

De Cesari, Chiara. 2010. "Creative Heritage: Palestinian Heritage NGOs and Defiant Arts of Government." *American Anthropologist* 112 (4): 625–37.

Dery, Mark, ed. 1994. *Flame Wars: The Discourse of Cyberculture*. Durham, N.C.: Duke University Press.

Descola, Philippe, and Marshall David Sahlins. 2014. *Beyond Nature and Culture*. Translated by Janet Lloyd. Paperback edition. Chicago: University of Chicago Press.

Despret, Vinciane. 2004. "The Body We Care For: Figures of Anthropo-Zoo-Genesis." *Body and Society* 10 (2–3): 111–34. https://doi.org/10.1177/1357034X04042938.

Dierendonck, Machteld C. van, and Michiel F. Wallis de Vries. 1996. "Ungulate Reintroductions: Experiences with the Takhi or Przewalski Horse (*Equus ferus przewalskii*) in Mongolia." *Conservation Biology* 10 (3): 728–40.

Dirksen, Rebecca. 2019. "Haiti's Drums and Trees: Facing Loss of the Sacred." *Ethnomusicology* 63 (1): 43–77. https://doi.org/10.5406/ethnomusicology.63.1.0043.

Dulmaa, A., and O. Shagdarsuren. 1972. *BNMAU-Yn Agnuuryn Am'tad Ba An Khamgaalal*. Ulaanbaatar: BNMAU Shinjlekh Ukhaany Akademi Biologiin Ukhaany Khureelen.

El Benni, Nadja, and Sophie Reviron. 2009. "Geographical Indications: Review of Seven Case-Studies World Wide." NCCR Trade Working Paper. January.

Eliade, Mircea. 1964. *Shamanism: Archaic Techniques of Ecstasy*. Bollingen Series 76. Princeton, N.J.: Princeton University Press.

Feld, Steven. 1996. "Waterfalls of Song: An Acoustemology of Place Resounding in Bosavi, Papua New Guinea." In *Senses of Place*, edited by Steven Feld and Keith Basso, 91–135. Santa Fe, N.M.: School of Advanced Research Press.

Fereidouni, Sasan, Graham L. Freimanis, Mukhit Orynbayev, Paolo Ribeca, John Flannery, Donald P. King, Steffen Zuther, et al. 2019. "Mass Die-Off of Saiga Antelopes, Kazakhstan, 2015." *Emerging Infectious Diseases* 25 (6): 1169–76. https://doi.org/10.3201/eid2506.180990.

Fernández-Giménez, María E., Niah H. Venable, Jay Angerer, Steven R. Fassnacht, Robin S. Reid, and J. Khishigbayar. 2017. "Exploring Linked Ecological and Cul-

tural Tipping Points in Mongolia." *Anthropocene* 17 (March): 46–69. https://doi
.org/10.1016/j.ancene.2017.01.003.

Fernando, Mayanthi. 2022. "Uncanny Ecologies." *Comparative Studies of South
Asia, Africa and the Middle East* 42 (3): 568–83. https://doi.org/10.1215/1089201X
-10148233.

Fijn, Natasha. 2011. *Living with Herds: Human-Animal Coexistence in Mongolia.* New
York: Cambridge University Press.

Fijn, Natasha. 2015. "The Domestic and the Wild in the Mongolian Horse and the
Takhi." In *Taxonomic Tapestries,* edited by Alison M. Behie and Marc F. Oxenham,
279–98. The Threads of Evolutionary, Behavioural and Conservation Research.
Canberra: Australian National University Press. http://www.jstor.org/stable/j
.ctt169wd9c.17.

Fusco, John, dir. 2014. *Marco Polo.* Netflix.

Gee, Jonon, and Bayaraa. 2011. *Миний Нутгийг Надад Улдээ.* Mongolz.

Gill, Victoria. 2018. "Chernobyl's Przewalski's Horses Are Poached for Meat." *BBC
Nature,* April 27, 2018.

Ginsburg, Tom. 1995. "Political Reform in Mongolia: Between Russia and China."
Asian Survey 35 (5): 459–71. https://doi.org/10.2307/2645748.

Giraldo Herrera, César Enrique. 2018. *Microbes and Other Shamanic Beings.* Cham:
Palgrave Macmillan.

Govindrajan, Radhika. 2018. *Animal Intimacies: Interspecies Relatedness in India's Central Himalayas.* Animal Lives. Chicago: University of Chicago Press.

Graham, Brian. 2002. "Heritage as Knowledge: Capital or Culture?" *Urban Studies*
39 (5–6): 1003–17.

Grewell, Greg. 2001. "Colonizing the Universe: Science Fictions Then, Now, and in
the (Imagined) Future." *Rocky Mountain Review of Language and Literature* 55 (2):
25. https://doi.org/10.2307/1348255.

Gün-Aajav, Ayurzana. 2010. *Бөөгийн Домог.* Ulaanbaatar: Mönkhiin Üseg Group.

Hahn, Tomie. 2007. *Sensational Knowledge: Embodying Culture through Japanese
Dance.* Middletown, Conn.: Wesleyan University Press.

Hamayon, Roberte. 1990. *La Chasse à l'âme: Esquisse d'une Théorie Du Chamanisme
Sibérien.* Mémoires de La Société d'Ethnologie 1. Nanterre.

Handler, Richard. 1988. *Nationalism and the Politics of Culture in Quebec.* New Directions in Anthropological Writing. Madison: University of Wisconsin Press.

Hanegraaff, Wouter J. 1998. *New Age Religion and Western Culture: Esotericism in the
Mirror of Secular Thought.* SUNY Series, Western Esoteric Traditions. Albany, N.Y.:
State University of New York Press.

Haraway, Donna Jeanne. 2003. *The Companion Species Manifesto: Dogs, People, and
Significant Otherness.* Paradigm 8. Chicago: Prickly Paradigm Press.

Haraway, Donna Jeanne. 2008. *When Species Meet.* Posthumanities 3. Minneapolis:
University of Minnesota Press.

Harner, Michael J. 1990. *The Way of the Shaman.* 10th ed. San Francisco: Harper & Row.

Hartigan, John. 2020. *Shaving the Beasts: Wild Horses and Ritual in Spain*. Minneapolis: University of Minnesota Press.

Harvey, David. 1989. *The Condition of Postmodernity: An Enquiry into the Origins of Cultural Change*. Cambridge, Mass.: Blackwell.

Harvey, David. 2005. *A Brief History of Neoliberalism*. Oxford: Oxford University Press.

Hasenkopf, Christa. 2012. "Clearing the Air." *World Policy Journal* 29 (1): 82–90. https://doi.org/10.1177/0740277512443805.

High, Mette M. 2017. *Fear and Fortune: Spirit Worlds and Emerging Economies in the Mongolian Gold Rush*. Ithaca, N.Y.: Cornell University Press.

Hirsch, Francine. 2005. *Empire of Nations: Ethnographic Knowledge and the Making of the Soviet Union*. Culture and Society after Socialism. Ithaca, N.Y.: Cornell University Press.

Hood, Mantle. 1960. "The Challenge of 'Bi-Musicality.'" *Ethnomusicology* 4 (2): 55. https://doi.org/10.2307/924263.

Huh, Kwon. 2016. "Intangible Cultural Heritage Safeguarding Efforts in Mongolia: In Collaboration with Mongolian National Commission for UNESCO. International Information and Networking Centre for Intangible Cultural Heritage in the Asia-Pacific Region under the Auspices of UNESCO." Report in possession of author.

Humphrey, Caroline. 1992. "The Moral Authority of the Past in Post-Socialist Mongolia." *Religion, State and Society* 20 (3–4): 375–89. https://doi.org/10.1080/09637499208431566.

Humphrey, Caroline. 1995. "Chiefly and Shamanist Landscapes in Mongolia." In *The Anthropology of Landscape: Perspectives on Place and Space*, edited by Eric Hirsch and Michael O'Hanlon, 135–62. Oxford: Oxford University Press.

Humphrey, Caroline, and Ujeed Hürelbaatar. 2013. *A Monastery in Time: The Making of Mongolian Buddhism*. Chicago: University of Chicago Press.

Humphrey, Caroline, and David Sneath. 1999. *The End of Nomadism? Society, State, and the Environment in Inner Asia*. Durham, N.C.: Duke University Press.

Hutchins, K. G. 2019. "Like a Lullaby: Song as Herding Tool in Rural Mongolia." *Journal of Ethnobiology* 39 (3): 445–59. https://doi.org/10.2993/0278-0771-39.3.445.

Hutchins, K. G. 2020. "The Melodious Hoofbeat: Ungulate Rhythms in the Post-Socialist Conservatory." *Inner Asia* 22 (2): 217–36. https://doi.org/10.1163/22105018-12340148.

Hutchins, K. G. 2021. "With Each Pass, Another Stone: Ovoo at the Heart of Heritage, Environment, and Conflict." *Études Mongoles et Sibériennes, Centrasiatiques et Tibétaines*, no. 52. https://doi.org/10.4000/emscat.5165.

Ingold, Tim. 1988. *Hunters, Pastoralists and Ranchers: Reindeer Economies and Their Transformations*. Cambridge: Cambridge University Press. https://doi.org/10.1017/CBO9780511558047.

Ingold, Tim. 2000. *The Perception of the Environment: Essays on Livelihood, Dwelling and Skill*. London: Routledge.

Irvine, Richard D. G. 2018. "Seeing Environmental Violence in Deep Time." *Environmental Humanities* 10 (1): 257–72. https://doi.org/10.1215/22011919-4385562.

Isono, Fujiko. 1976. "The Mongolian Revolution of 1921." *Modern Asian Studies* 10 (3): 375–94.

Ivarsdotter, Anna. 2004. "'And the Cattle Follow Her, for They Know Her Voice': On Communication between Women and Cattle in Scandinavian Pastures." *Proceedings from PECUS. Man and Animal in Antiquity*, 150–53.

Jackson, Sara L. 2015. "Dusty Roads and Disconnections: Perceptions of Dust from Unpaved Mining Roads in Mongolia's South Gobi Province." *Geoforum* 66 (November): 94–105. https://doi.org/10.1016/j.geoforum.2015.09.010.

Janes, Craig R., and Oyuntsetseg Chuluundorj. 2015. *Making Disasters: Climate Change, Neoliberal Governance, and Livelihood Insecurity on the Mongolian Steppe.* Resident Scholar Series. Santa Fe, N.M.: School for Advanced Research Press.

Jantsannorov, Natsagiin. 2006. *Хөгжим Цаг Ye.* Ulaanbaatar: ADMON Press.

Johnson, Anna. 1984. "Voice Physiology and Ethnomusicology: Physiological and Acoustical Studies of the Swedish Herding Song." *Yearbook for Traditional Music* 16:42–66. https://doi.org/10.2307/768202.

Kaczensky, Petra, Oyunsaikhan Ganbataar, Nanjid Altansukh, Namtar Enkhsaikhan, Christian Stauffer, and Chris Walzer. 2011. "The Danger of Having All Your Eggs in One Basket—Winter Crash of the Re-Introduced Przewalski's Horses in the Mongolian Gobi." Edited by Georges Chapouthier. *PLoS ONE* 6 (12): e28057. https://doi.org/10.1371/journal.pone.0028057.

Kaczensky, Petra, Oyunsaikhan Ganbataar, Henrik von Wehrden, Namtar Enksaikhan, Lkhagvasuren Davaa, and Chris Walzer. 2007. "Przewalski's Horse (*Equus ferus przewalskii*) Re-Introduction in the Great Gobi B Strictly Protected Area: From Species to Ecosystem Conservation." *Mongolian Journal of Biological Sciences* 5 (1–2). https://doi.org/10.22353/mjbs.2007.05.03.

Kahn, Paul, and Francis Woodman Cleaves. 1998. *The Secret History of the Mongols: The Origin of Chinghis Khan; An Adaptation of the Yüan Ch'ao Pi Shih, Based Primarily on the English Translation by Francis Woodman Cleaves.* Expanded ed. C & T Asian Culture Series. Boston: Cheng & Tsui.

Kaplonski, C. 2014. *The Lama Question: Violence, Sovereignty, and Exception in Early Socialist Mongolia.* Honolulu: University of Hawai'i Press.

Kassenova, Togzhan. 2022. *Atomic Steppe: How Kazakhstan Gave up the Bomb.* Stanford, Calif: Stanford University Press.

Kehoe, Alice B. 1996. "Eliade and Hultkrantz: The European Primitivism Tradition." *American Indian Quarterly* 20 (3–4): 377–92. https://doi.org/10.2307/1185783.

Khaidav, P., and B. Chagnaadorj. 1969. *BNMAU-Yn An Am'tad.* Ulaanbaatar: Ulsyn Khevleliin Gazar.

Khangalov, Matvei. 1890. *Новые Матеріалы о Шаманствѣ и Бурят.* Vol. 1. Irkutsk: *Тип. К.И. Витковской.*

Khustain Baigaliin Tsogtsolbort Gazar ("*Хустайн байгалийн цогцолборт газар*")." n.d. Accessed March 9, 2020. https://www.hustai.mn/wp/.

King, S. R. B. 2002. "Home Range and Habitat Use of Free-Ranging Przewalski Horses at Hustai National Park, Mongolia." *Applied Animal Behaviour Science* 78 (2–4): 103–13. https://doi.org/10.1016/S0168-1591(02)00087-4.

Kirshenblatt-Gimblett, Barbara. 1995. "Theorizing Heritage." *Ethnomusicology* 39 (3): 367–80. https://doi.org/10.2307/924627.

Kirshenblatt-Gimblett, Barbara. 2004. "Intangible Heritage as Metacultural Production." *Museum International* 56 (1–2): 52–65. https://doi.org/10.1111/j.1350-0775 .2004.00458.x.

Kivelson, Valerie A. 2006. *Cartographies of Tsardom: The Land and Its Meanings in Seventeenth-Century Russia.* Ithaca, N.Y.: Cornell University Press.

Klinger, Julie Michelle. 2017. *Rare Earth Frontiers: From Terrestrial Subsoils to Lunar Landscapes.* Ithaca, N.Y.: Cornell University Press.

Kogan, Lori R., Regina Schoenfeld-Tacher, and Allen A. Simon. 2012. "Behavioral Effects of Auditory Stimulation on Kenneled Dogs." *Journal of Veterinary Behavior* 7 (5): 268–75. https://doi.org/10.1016/j.jveb.2011.11.002.

Kohn, Eduardo. 2013. *How Forests Think: Toward an Anthropology beyond the Human.* Berkeley: University of California Press.

Kopack, Robert A. 2019. "Rocket Wastelands in Kazakhstan: Scientific Authoritarianism and the Baikonur Cosmodrome." *Annals of the American Association of Geographers* 109 (2): 556–67. https://doi.org/10.1080/24694452.2018.1507817.

Kuromiya, Hiroaki. 2014. "Stalin's Great Terror and the Asian Nexus." *Europe-Asia Studies* 66 (5): 775–93.

Latour, Bruno. 2005. *Reassembling the Social: An Introduction to Actor-Network-Theory.* Clarendon Lectures in Management Studies. Oxford: Oxford University Press.

Lefebvre, Henri. 2004. *Rhythmanalysis: Space, Time, and Everyday Life.* London: Continuum.

Legrain, Laurent. 2016. "Drunkards and Singers: A Mongolian Battle of Sounds." *Journal of Ethnology and Folkloristics* 10 (2): 65–80. https://doi.org/10.1515/jef -2016-0011.

Lempert, William. 2014. "Decolonizing Encounters of the Third Kind: Alternative Futuring in Native Science Fiction Film." *Visual Anthropology Review* 30 (2): 164– 76. https://doi.org/10.1111/var.12046.

Lepofsky, Dana. 2009. "The Past, Present, and Future of Traditional Resource and Environmental Management." *Journal of Ethnobiology* 29 (2): 161–66. https://doi .org/10.2993/0278-0771-29.2.161.

Levin, Dan. 2009. "Shamans' Spirits Crowd Air of Mongolian Capital." *New York Times,* July 10, 2009. https://www.nytimes.com/2009/07/11/world/asia/11iht-shaman.html.

Levin, Theodore, and Valentina Ûr'evna Suzukej. 2006. *Where Rivers and Mountains Sing: Sound, Music, and Nomadism in Tuva and Beyond.* Bloomington: Indiana University Press.

Levy, Ariel. 2016. "The Drug of Choice for the Age of Kale: How Ayahuasca, an Ancient Amazonian Hallucinogenic Brew, Became the Latest Trend in Brooklyn and

Silicon Valley." *New Yorker*, September 12, 2016. https://www.newyorker.com/magazine/2016/09/12/the-ayahuasca-boom-in-the-u-s.

Linden, Kenneth E. 2021. "Animals, Socialism, and Continuity: Wolf Hunting in the Mongolian People's Republic." *Inner Asia* 23 (2): 257–84. https://doi.org/10.1163/22105018-12340174.

Lowenthal, David. 1996. *Possessed by the Past: The Heritage Crusade and the Spoils of History*. New York: Free Press.

Luvsannorov, Erdenechimeg. 2015. *Ayalguut Magtaal*. Ulaanbaatar: Öngöt Khevlel.

Madison Pískatá, Jessica. 2018. "Golden Mountain, Iron Heap: A Poetic Ethnography of Extraction in Eastern Mongolia." *AURA Working Papers* 3:46–52.

Madison Pískatá, Jessica. 2021a. "'In Any Crystalline Land': The Poetics of Human/Mineral Worlds in Eastern Mongolia." Santa Cruz: University of California, Santa Cruz.

Madison Pískatá, Jessica. 2021b. "On Offering and Forgiveness at Altan Ovoo's National Tahilga." *Études Mongoles et Sibériennes, Centrasiatiques et Tibétaines*, no. 52 (December). https://doi.org/10.4000/emscat.5119.

Madison Pískatá, Jessica. 2024. "Provincializing Energy in the Mongolian Gobi." *SSRC Intersections* (blog). October 1, 2024. https://intersections.ssrc.org/projects/provincializing-energy-in-the-mongolian-gobi/.

Marchina, Charlotte. 2019. *Nomad's land: éleveurs, animaux et paysages chez les peuples mongols*. Bruxelles: Zones sensibles.

Marsh, Peter K. 2009. *The Horse-Head Fiddle and the Cosmopolitan Reimagination of Tradition in Mongolia*. Current Research in Ethnomusicology. New York: Routledge.

Martinelli, Dario. 2009. *Of Birds, Whales, and Other Musicians: An Introduction to Zoomusicology*. Approaches to Postmodernity, v. 3. Scranton, Pa.: University of Scranton Press.

Massumi, Brian. 1995. "The Autonomy of Affect." *Cultural Critique*, no. 31, 83–109. https://doi.org/10.2307/1354446.

Meskell, Lynn. 2002. "Negative Heritage and Past Mastering in Archaeology." *Anthropological Quarterly* 75 (3): 557–74.

Mijiddorj, Tserennadmid Nadia, Ariell Ahearn, Charudutt Mishra, and Bazartseren Boldgiv. 2019. "Gobi Herders' Decision-Making and Risk Management under Changing Climate." *Human Ecology* 47 (5): 785–94. https://doi.org/10.1007/s10745-019-00112-9.

Mohr, Erna. 1971. *The Asiatic Wild Horse*. 2nd ed. London: J. A. Allen.

Munkhjargal, Munkhdavaa, Gansukh Yadamsuren, Jambaljav Yamkhin, and Lucas Menzel. 2020. "The Combination of Wildfire and Changing Climate Triggers Permafrost Degradation in the Khentii Mountains, Northern Mongolia." *Atmosphere* 11 (2): 155. https://doi.org/10.3390/atmos11020155.

Myadar, Orhon. 2011. "Imaginary Nomads: Deconstructing the Representation of Mongolia as a Land of Nomads." *Inner Asia* 13 (2): 335–62.

Myagmarsüren, Dorjdagva. 2013. *Mongol Urtyn Duu, Tüüniig Övlögchid*. Edited by Enebish Jambal and Alimaa Ayushjav. Ulaanbaatar, Mongolia: International Institute for the Study of Nomadic Civilizations.

National Statistics Office of Mongolia (*Үндэсний Статистикийн Хороо*). n.d. "*Хүн Ам.*" Accessed March 19, 2020. https://1212.mn/en.

Nisvanis. 2006. *Нисдэг Таваг*. Track 8. *Нисдэг Таваг*. Ulaanbaatar, Mongolia: Hi-Fi Media Group.

Nkrumah, Kwame. 1976. *Neo-Colonialism: The Last Stage of Imperialism*. 6th ed. New World Paperbacks. New York: International Publishers.

Nollman, Jim. 1999. *The Charged Border: Where Whales and Humans Meet*. New York: Henry Holt.

Parreñas, Juno Salazar. 2018. *Decolonizing Extinction: The Work of Care in Orangutan Rehabilitation*. Experimental Futures: Technological Lives, Scientific Arts, Anthropological Voices. Durham, N.C.: Duke University Press.

Pedersen, Morten Axel, ed. 2011. *Not Quite Shamans: Spirit Worlds and Political Lives in Northern Mongolia*. Culture and Society after Socialism. Ithaca, N.Y.: Cornell University Press.

Pegg, Carole. 2001. *Mongolian Music, Dance, and Oral Narrative: Performing Diverse Identities*. Seattle: University of Washington Press.

Posthumus, David C. 2018. *All My Relatives: Exploring Lakota Ontology, Belief, and Ritual*. New Visions in Native American and Indigenous Studies. Lincoln: University of Nebraska Press.

Povinelli, Elizabeth A. 2016. *Geontologies: A Requiem to Late Liberalism*. Durham, N.C.: Duke University Press.

Redford, Kent. 1991. "The Ecologically Noble Savage." *Cultural Survival Quarterly* 15:46–48.

Rees, Helen. 1998. "'Authenticity' and the Foreign Audience for Traditional Music in Southwest China." *Journal of Musicological Research* 17 (2): 135–61. https://doi.org/10.1080/01411899808574744.

Rice, Timothy. 1996. "Traditional and Modern Methods of Learning and Teaching Music in Bulgaria." *Research Studies in Music Education* 7 (1): 1–12. https://doi.org/10.1177/1321103X9600700101.

Rice, Timothy. 2003. "The Ethnomusicology of Music Learning and Teaching." *College Music Symposium* 43:65–85.

Rieder, John. 2008. *Colonialism and the Emergence of Science Fiction*. The Wesleyan Early Classics of Science Fiction Series. Middletown, Conn: Wesleyan University Press.

Rifkin, Mark. 2017. *Beyond Settler Time: Temporal Sovereignty and Indigenous Self-Determination*. Durham, N.C.: Duke University Press.

Rofel, Lisa. 1999. *Other Modernities: Gendered Yearnings in China after Socialism*. Berkeley: University of California Press.

Rosaldo, Renato. 1989. "Imperialist Nostalgia." *Representations* 26 (April): 107–22. https://doi.org/10.2307/2928525.

Rosen, Arlene M., Thomas C. Hart, Jennifer Farquhar, Joan S. Schneider, and Tserendagva Yadmaa. 2019. "Holocene Vegetation Cycles, Land-Use, and Human Adaptations to Desertification in the Gobi Desert of Mongolia." *Vegetation History and Archaeobotany* 28 (3): 295–309. https://doi.org/10.1007/s00334-018-0710-y.

Rothenberg, David. 2008. "Whale Music: Anatomy of an Interspecies Duet." *Leonardo Music Journal* 18:47–53.

Ryder, Oliver A. 1993. "Przewalski's Horse: Prospects for Reintroduction into the Wild." *Conservation Biology* 7 (1): 13–15.

Said, Edward W. 1979. *Orientalism*. New York: Vintage Books.

Said, Edward W. 1994. *Culture and Imperialism*. New York: Vintage Books.

Sampildendev, L. and K. N. Yatskovskoj. 1984. *Монгол Ардын Уртын Дуу*. Ulaanbaatar: Ulsyn Khevleliin Gazar.

Schroer, Sara. 2018. "Breeding with Birds of Prey." In *Domestication Gone Wild: Politics and Practices of Multispecies Relations*, edited by Heather Anne Swanson, Marianne E. Lien, and Gro Ween, 34–49. Durham, N.C.: Duke University Press.

Seeger, Anthony. 1987. *Why Suyá Sing: A Musical Anthropology of an Amazonian People*. Cambridge Studies in Ethnomusicology. Cambridge: Cambridge University Press.

Shagdar, Enkhbayar. 2007. "Neo-Liberal 'Shock Therapy' Policy During the Mongolian Economic Transition." *ERINA Discussion Paper* 0703e (April).

Sheehy, Dennis, and Daalkhaijav Damiran. 2012. *Assessment of Mongolian Rangeland Condition and Trend (1997–2009)*. World Bank and the Netherlands-Mongolia Trust Fund for Environmental Reform.

Shouse, Eric. 2005. "Feeling, Emotion, Affect." *M/C Journal* 8 (6). https://doi.org/10.5204/mcj.2443.

Simonett, Helena. 2015. "Of Human and Non-Human Birds: Indigenous Music Making and Sentient Ecology in Northwestern Mexico." In *Current Directions in Ecomusicology: Music, Nature, Environment*, edited by Aaron Allen and Kevin Dawe, 99–108. New York: Routledge.

Sneath, David. 2003. "Lost in the Post: Technologies of Imagination, and the Soviet Legacy in Post-Socialist Mongolia." *Inner Asia* 5 (1): 39–52.

Sneath, David. 2014. "Nationalising Civilisational Resources: Sacred Mountains and Cosmopolitical Ritual in Mongolia." *Asian Ethnicity* 15 (4): 458–72. https://doi.org/10.1080/14631369.2014.939330.

Snowdon, Charles T., David Teie, and Megan Savage. 2015. "Cats Prefer Species-Appropriate Music." *Applied Animal Behaviour Science* 166 (May): 106–11. https://doi.org/10.1016/j.applanim.2015.02.012.

Spinoza, Benedictus de, and E. M. Curley. 1985. *The Collected Works of Spinoza*. Princeton, N.J.: Princeton University Press.

Strathern, Marilyn. 1980. "No Nature; No Culture: The Hagen Case." In *Nature, Culture, Gender*, edited by C MacCormack and Marilyn Strathern, 174–222. Cambridge: Cambridge University Press.

Swanson, Heather Anne, Marianne E. Lien, and Gro Ween, eds. 2018. *Domestication Gone Wild: Politics and Practices of Multispecies Relations*. Durham, N.C.: Duke University Press.

Terbish, Baasanjav. 2023. "The Cat in Mongolian Society: A Good, Bad and Ugly Animal." *Central Asian Survey* 42 (3): 561–576. https://doi.org/10.1080/02634937.2023.2201306.

The HU. 2019. *The Gereg.* Dashka Productions.

Thompson, Niobe. 2008. *Settlers on the Edge: Identity and Modernization on Russia's Arctic Frontier.* Vancouver: University of British Columbia Press.

Titon, Jeff Todd. 2009. "Economy, Ecology, and Music: An Introduction." *World of Music* 51 (1): 5–15.

Trouillot, Michel-Rolph. 2003. *Global Transformations: Anthropology and the Modern World.* New York: Palgrave Macmillan.

Tsing, A. 2013. "More-than-Human Sociality: A Call for Critical Description." In *Anthropology and Nature,* edited by Kirsten Hastrup, 27–42. New York: Routledge.

Tsing, Anna. 2012. "Unruly Edges: Mushrooms as Companion Species: For Donna Haraway." *Environmental Humanities* 1 (1): 141–54. https://doi.org/10.1215/22011919-3610012.

Tsing, Anna Lowenhaupt. 2015. *The Mushroom at the End of the World: On the Possibility of Life in Capitalist Ruins.* Princeton, N.J.: Princeton University Press.

Tucker, Joshua. 2016. "Nature's Sonorous Politics: Music, Ecology, and Indigenous Activism in Andean Peru." *Revista: Harvard Review of Latin America* 15:73–76.

Tumurtogoo, Anand, and Jake Pearson. 2019. "Donald Trump Jr. Went to Mongolia, Got Special Treatment from the Government and Killed an Endangered Sheep." *ProPublica,* December 11, 2019.

Turner, Nancy J., Marianne Boelscher Ignace, and Ronald Ignace. 2000. "Traditional Ecological Knowledge and Wisdom of Aboriginal Peoples in British Columbia." *Ecological Applications* 10 (5): 1275–87. https://doi.org/10.1890/1051-0761(2000)010[1275:TEKAWO]2.0.CO;2.

Uetake, K., J. F. Hurnik, and L. Johnson. 1997. "Effect of Music on Voluntary Approach of Dairy Cows to an Automatic Milking System." *Applied Animal Behaviour Science* 53 (3): 175–82. https://doi.org/10.1016/S0168-1591(96)01159-8.

UNESCO. 1972. *Convention Concerning the Protection of the World Cultural and Natural Heritage.* 17th General Conference of the United Nations Educational, Scientific and Cultural Organization, Paris, France. http://whc.unesco.org/archive/convention-en.pdf.

UNESCO. 2003. *Basic Texts of the 2003 Convention for the Safeguarding of the Intangible Cultural Heritage.* Paris, France. https://ich.unesco.org/doc/src/2003_Convention_Basic_Texts-_2018_version-EN.pdf.

UNESCO. 2004. *Orkhon Valley Cultural Landscape Nomination File.* Report of the 28th Session of the World Heritage Committee. https://whc.unesco.org/uploads/nominations/1081rev.pdf.

UNESCO. 2015a. *Great Burkhan Khaldun Mountain and Its Surrounding Sacred Landscape Nomination File.* https://whc.unesco.org/uploads/nominations/1440.pdf.

UNESCO. 2015b. *Sacred Mountains of Mongolia Nomination File.* https://whc.unesco.org/en/tentativelists/6068/.

UNESCO. 2017. *12th Session, Intergovernmental Committee for the Safeguarding of the Intangible Cultural Heritage.* Jeju Island, Republic of Korea. https://ich.unesco.org/en/12com.

UNESCO. 2018. *Operational Directives for the Implementation of the Convention for the Safeguarding of the Intangible Cultural Heritage*. Paris, France. https://ich.unesco .org/doc/src/ICH-Operational_Directives-7.GA-PDF-EN.pdf.

Van Dooren, Thom, and Deborah Bird Rose. 2012. "Storied-Places in a Multispecies City." *Humanimalia* 3 (2): 1–27. https://doi.org/10.52537/humanimalia.10046.

Verdery, Katherine. 1996. *What Was Socialism, and What Comes Next?* Princeton Studies in Culture/Power/History. Princeton, N.J.: Princeton University Press.

Vitebsky, Piers. 1995. *The Shaman*. Living Wisdom. London: Macmillan.

Voyles, Traci Brynne. 2015. *Wastelanding: Legacies of Uranium Mining in Navajo Country*. Minneapolis: University of Minnesota Press.

Wakefield, Simon, John Knowles, Waltraut Zimmermann, and Machteld Dierendonck. 2002. "Status and Action Plan for the Przewalski's Horse (*Equus ferus przewalskii*)." In *Equids: Zebras, Asses and Horses; Status Survey and Conservation Action Plan*, edited by Patricia D. Moehlman, 82–92. Gland, Switzerland: International Union for Conservation of Nature.

Wallace, Vesna. 2012. "Surviving Modernity in Mongolia." In *Mongolians after Socialism: Politics, Economy, Religion*, edited by Bruce M Knauft, Richard Taupier, and Lkham Purevjav, 89–100. Ulaanbaatar: Admon Press.

Weber, Max. 1958. *The Protestant Ethic and the Spirit of Capitalism*. Translated by T. Parsons. New York: Charles Scribner's Sons.

Weber, Max, Guenther Roth, and Claus Wittich. 1978. *Economy and Society: An Outline of Interpretive Sociology*. Berkeley: University of California Press.

Wells, D. L., L. Graham, and P. G. Hepper. 2002. "The Influence of Auditory Stimulation on the Behaviour of Dogs Housed in a Rescue Shelter." *Animal Welfare* 11 (4): 385–93. https://doi.org/10.1017/S0962728600025112.

Willerslev, Rane. 2007. *Soul Hunters: Hunting, Animism, and Personhood among the Siberian Yukaghirs*. Berkeley: University of California Press.

Wong, Chuen-Fung. 2019. "'Original Ecology' Style of China's Minority Performing Arts: Examples from Uyghur Music." In *Chinese Shock of the Anthropocene*, edited by Kwai-Cheung Lo and Jessica Yeung, 203–23. Singapore: Springer Singapore. https://doi.org/10.1007/978-981-13-6685-7_10.

Wong, Deborah. 2008. "Moving: From Performance to Performative Ethnography and Back Again." In *Shadows in the Field: New Perspective for Fieldwork in Ethnomusicology*, edited by Gregory F. Barz and Timothy J. Cooley, 76–89. New York: Oxford University Press.

Yi, Li-Na, and Teng-Fei Shi. 2016. "Study on the Urbanization of Mongolian State 'Herdsman Workers': Field Survey of 'Ger Horool' in Ulaanbaatar." *Journal of Inner Mongolia University for Nationalities* 42 (2): 33–38.

Yoon, Sunmin. 2013. "Remains and Renewals." *Mongolian Studies* 35:119–31.

Yoon, Sunmin. 2019. "What's in the Song? Urtyn Duu as Sonic 'Ritual' among Mongolian Herder-Singers." *MUSICultures* 45 (1–2). https://journals.lib.unb.ca/index .php/MC/article/view/28936.

Zharkikh, Tatjana, and Nataliya Yasynetska. 2009. "Ten Years of Development of the Przewalski Horse Population in the Chernobyl Exclusive Zone." *Equus*, 139–56.

Zharkikh, Tatjana, Nataliya Yasynetska, and Nataliya Zvegintsova. 2002. "Przewalski Horse in the Zone of Chernobyl Nuclear Power." *Gazella* 29 (January): 93–111.

Znamenski, Andrei A. 2007. *The Beauty of the Primitive: Shamanism and the Western Imagination.* Oxford: Oxford University Press.

Zul, Zugeerbai, and Hyunwook Cheng. 2022. "An Inefficacious Shock Therapy? A Critical Analysis of Mongolian Neoliberal Reforms." *Mongolian Journal of International Affairs* 23 (December): 40–54. https://doi.org/10.5564/mjia.v23i1.2423.

INDEX

ABOUT THE AUTHOR

K. G. Hutchins is a cultural anthropologist interested in the intersection of music and the environment. He is a visiting professor in the Department of Anthropology at Oberlin College. His research focuses on the roles that nonhuman animals, spirits, and other beings can play in cultural heritage, particularly in Mongolia and Southern Appalachia. His first book, *A Song for the Horses*, draws on research with nomads and musicians he has undertaken since 2010.